WHY THE
RICH
ARE GETTING
RICHER

What Is
Financial
Education
...Really?

ROBERT T. KIYOSAKI

Author of the International Bestseller *Rich Dad Poor Dad*

TOM WHEELWRIGHT, CPA • ADJUVANT
Author of the Bestseller *Tax-Free Wealth*

PLATA®
PUBLISHING

Published by Plata Publishing, LLC

CASHFLOW, Rich Dad, and CASHFLOW Quadrant are registered trademarks of CASHFLOW Technologies, Inc.

are registered trademarks of CASHFLOW Technologies, Inc.

Cone of Learning from Dale. Audio-Visual Methods in Teaching, 1E. © 1969 South-Western, a part of Cengage, Inc. Reproduced by permission. www.cengage.com/permissions

Plata Publishing, LLC
4330 N. Civic Center Plaza
Suite 100
Scottsdale, AZ 85251
(480) 998-6971

Visit our website: RichDad.com
Printed in the United States of America

ISBN 978-1-61268-088-0

012018

DEDICATION

This book is dedicated to the students and faculty
of St. Andrews College,
the Diocesan School For Girls, and Rhodes University
in Grahamstown, South Africa.

In July of 2016,
Tom Wheelwright, CPA and Rich Dad Advisor on taxes, and I
traveled to South Africa to teach this fabulous group
of young people, teachers, and entrepreneurs.

For Tom and me, it was a life-changing event.

This book is dedicated to them,
the students, teachers, and entrepreneurs
who are so committed to education in Africa and the world.

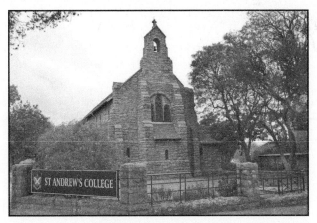

*St. Andrew's College was founded in 1855
in Grahamstown, South Africa*

RDTV

At the back of this book you will find
10 Video Lessons:

RDTV
Real Financial Education

Awaken Your Financial Genius
10 TV Lessons for You

"I wished I had learned this in school! I've had more than two decades of formal education, but was never taught about money in school. The learning environment—the discussions, the game play, and the *RDTV* lessons—opened my eyes to what I need to know and learn. Now I can make the changes I need to make in my life… changes that offer me a whole new world."

— Dr. Arthur Kaba | Medical Doctor

"I've played the *CASHFLOW game* 10 times in the past three months… and participated in discussions about the game and *RDTV's* 10 lessons. Today, I see a totally different world. Now I know what I *really* need to learn. Now I understand why the rich are getting richer."

— Marlon August | Two-time Olympian and Entrepreneur

> *"The issue of wealth and income inequality is the great moral issue of our time"*

— Senator Bernie Sanders, Socialist (D) Vermont
and 2016 Democratic Presidential Candidate

Two Points of View... Two Solutions

U.S Senator
Bernie Sanders

U.S President
Donald Trump

The growing gap between the rich and everyone else is a moral crisis and a social time bomb.

Bernie Sanders believes in *giving people fish*;
Donald Trump and I believe in teaching people to fish.

Although we do not agree with Bernie Sanders politically, we do agree with him in principle.

Our differences lie in the solution to this growing problem.

If you believe in *giving people fish*, this book is not for you.
If you believe in *teaching people to fish*, you may find this book interesting.

For Educators and Parents...

Why You Don't Need Money to Get Rich

Stanford University agrees with my rich dad—not my poor dad.

At age nine, I learned what Stanford University professor Tina Seelig wished she knew—at 20!

Academics and parents, please read this book. It supports Rich Dad's teaching methods for students who want to be entrepreneurs.

At age nine, my rich dad refused to pay me. He said, "If I pay you, you will think like an employee. I want you to think like an entrepreneur." His point: The rich don't work for money.

by Tina Seelig

BEFORE YOU
START THIS BOOK…
a word about the BONUS Sections

There are Bonus Sections at the
front and the back of this book.
They are included to supplement and reinforce
the importance of the messages in this book.

We've all heard the classic definition of insanity:
"… doing the same thing over and over again
and expecting different results."

**These Bonus sections are included to encourage you
to read and understand the contents of this book
and make changes… now.**

OBSOLETE ADVICE?

"Go to school, get a job, save money, get out of debt, and invest for the long-term in the stock market."

WHAT IS DIFFERENT?

Rich Dad Poor Dad • published 1997
Elementary School: Basic financial education

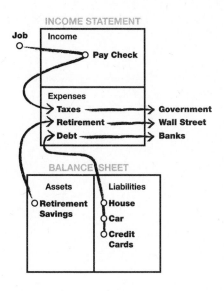

Rich Dad Poor Dad is about elementary financial education.

Financial education requires financial literacy: an understanding the words and numbers of money.

The two most important words in financial literacy are **cash flow**. The financial statement diagram here illustrates why the poor and middle class grow poorer. Without financial education, the poor and middle class are unable to control the cash that flows out of their pockets (see arrows) into the pockets of the government, banks, and Wall Street.

Why the Rich Are Getting Richer • published 2017
Graduate School: Advanced financial education

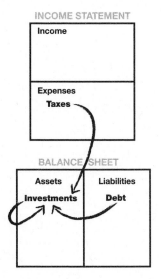

One reason why the rich are getting richer is because the rich have more control over their **cash flow**.

As the arrows in the diagram to the left illustrate, **the rich use their tax dollars** to acquire assets—rather than have their tax dollars flow to the government. Rather than use their money to acquire assets, **the rich use debt**, their banker's money, to buy assets.

And instead of sending their retirement savings to Wall Street, the rich continually reinvest their own money to acquire more assets.

To do this requires real financial education. Real financial education is what this book is about... really. *Why the Rich Are Getting Richer* is financial education for Rich Dad's graduate students.

Why "going to school" is an obsolete idea.

What does school teach you about money?

CAPITALISM, COMMUNISM, & EDUCATION

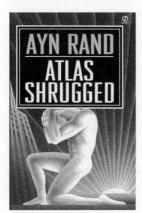

What did school teach you about money?

For most people, the answer is, "not much." If they did learn anything, what they learned was "Go to school, get a job, save money, buy a house, get out of debt, and invest for the long term in the stock market." That might have been great advice for the Industrial Age, but it's obsolete advice in the Information Age.

Globalization meant an end to high-paying jobs for blue-collar workers. Jobs moved to China, India, Mexico...

The rise of robots will mean the end of high-paying jobs for white-collar workers.

The Rise of Robots

Today, if jobs are not moving overseas, robots and artificial intelligence are replacing workers. Even highly-educated doctors, lawyers, and accountants are in the crosshairs of robots. Adidas just announced it would begin manufacturing shoes in Germany and the

United States, rather than China or Vietnam. And Foxconn, Apple's primary manufacturer, just announced it is ordering one million robots—to replace three million workers.

Students all over the world leave school, many deeply in student-loan debt—the most onerous of all debt—unable to find the mythical high-paying job that could amortize that student loan.

Robots do not need paychecks or raises, they work longer, do not need vacations, time off, medical benefits, or a retirement plan.

Savers Are Losers

Once upon a time, in the 1970s, a person with $1 million in savings, earned 15% interest or $150,000 a year. Back then, a person could live on $150,000 annually. Today, $1 million might earn 1.5% interest or $15,000 annually, hardly a living wage for a millionaire. Today, savers are the biggest losers.

Your House Is Not an Asset

And in 2008, approximately 10 million homeowners learned, first-hand, that their home was not an asset when the real estate market crashed and the mortgage on the property was greater than the resale value of the home.

McMansions, once the pride of the baby-boom generation, are today's *dog houses of real estate*. The kids and grandkids of boomers, the millennials, cannot afford their grandparents' "biggest asset"—nor do they want it.

As real estate taxes rise, prices of McMansions will continue to fall. Small and efficient will be better than big and obnoxious when it comes to housing.

And home prices are related to jobs. Robots do not need a home. Robots live at the office, 24/7.

Happy Birthday

Rich Dad Poor Dad was self-published 20 years ago on April 8, 1997, my 50th birthday. It was self-published because every editor working for the giant publishing houses was like my poor dad, a well-educated academic without much financial education.

My rich dad's lessons on financial education disturbed the editors' academic beliefs on money… and we all know how comforting our beliefs are, even if they're obsolete.

Today, 20 years later, my rich dad's lessons on money are truer and more disturbing than they were two decades ago. Today's savers are even bigger losers as interest rates drop below zero in many countries and robots continue to replace workers. Yet parents continue to advise their kids to do as they did: "Go to school, get a job, and save money."

Economics Is Not Financial Education

Academic types, in defense of their lack of financial education, often spit back, "I studied economics in school." Or "My child's school has a great economics program." A few academic name-droppers will mention famous economists such as John Maynard Keynes, Milton Friedman, Ludwig von Mises, or Friederich Hayek. These economists' theories may have held some water 50 years ago, but today their theories are leaking and the dam is about to burst.

Economic Philosophers

Rather than academic economists, I prefer to listen to two influential economic philosophers: Karl Marx, author of *The Communist Manifesto*, and Ayn Rand, author of *Atlas Shrugged*.

Ayn Rand

Ayn Rand was born in St. Petersburg, Russia in 1905 and witnessed the Russian revolution as a teenager. The Bolsheviks took her father's business and everything he had worked for. In 1926, she immigrated to New York City. Having experienced both Communism and Capitalism, her views on both economic systems are potent. Critical of Western economists and academics who live in theoretical bubbles she said: *"He is free to evade reality... but not free to avoid the abyss he refuses to see."*

It's said that Rand's heroes continually oppose "parasites," "looters," and "moochers" who demand the benefits of the heroes' labor. The *parasites*, *looters*, and *moochers* are proponents of high taxation, big labor, government ownership, government spending, government planning, regulation, and redistribution.

Looters are Rand's depiction of bureaucrats and government officials who confiscate others' earnings by the implicit threat of force—"at the point of a gun." They use force to take property from the people who "produced" or "earned" it.

Moochers, in Rand's depiction, are those unable to produce value themselves. Since they are incapable of producing, their scam is to demand others' earnings, the earnings of the producers, on behalf of the needy. In the name of the needy, they steal the wealth of producers to line their own pockets. They resent the talents of producers, and blather on about "moral right of people," while enabling "lawful" seizure by government.

As you know, the world is filled with non-producing moochers, looters, and parasites posing as "morally and intellectually superior do-gooders."

As the title implies, Atlas Shrugged poses the question: *What happens if the producers simply shrugged, stop producing and contributing, and go into hiding?*

Atlas Shrugged was published in 1957 and was initially attacked and criticized. Yet, as time passed, the book became a classic, with people stating, "After The Bible, Atlas Shrugged is the most important book in my life."

Karl Marx

Karl Marx was born in 1818 in Prussia, which today is Germany. He is known as a socialist and revolutionary, a man who influenced many of today's modern revolutionaries such as Vladimir Lenin, Mao Tse-tung, Fidel Castro, Hugo Chavez, and Che Guevara.

One of his more famous quotes is: *"Let the ruling classes tremble at a communist revolution. The proletarians have nothing to lose but their chains. They have a world to win. Workingmen of all countries, unite!"*

Marx's socialist views were so disturbing he was forced to move out of Europe and into England. In London, he found a job writing for the *New York Tribune*, where he found a receptive audience in America, writing about slavery, class struggle, and class consciousness.

Class Struggle

In overly simple terms, Marx defined class struggle as the conflict between the aristocracy, the bourgeois, and the proletariat. Definitions of these classes are:

Aristocracy: A ruling class that inherits wealth, special privileges, and title, typically a monarchy.

Bourgeois: An adjective relating to or typical of the middle class. If someone says, "Oh how bourgeois!" it is probably an insult, meaning you're preoccupied with middle class small-mindedness.

Marx referred to the bourgeois as people preoccupied with material possessions, yet lacking much drive and ambition, comfortable with being comfortable.

Proletariat: a. A class of wage-earners possessing neither capital nor means of production; b. People who sell their labor to earn a living; c. The poorest class of working people.

Aristocrats

During the Agrarian Age, it was the kings and queens, the aristocrats, who owned the land. The word *peasants* is derived from the French words, *pays* and *sants*—people who worked the land, but did not own the land. The words *real estate*, in Spanish, mean *royal estate*.

During the Industrial Age, the aristocracy was industrial giants such as Henry Ford, John D. Rockefeller, and JP Morgan. Ford produced cars, Rockefeller produced the gasoline, and Morgan produced the money.

In the Information Age, the new aristocracy is tech wizards who control cyber-real estate… people such as Apple co-founder Steve Jobs, Jeff Bezos of Amazon, and Sergey Brin and Larry Page of Google.

During the Agrarian Age, the rich were called aristocracy. Today they are called capitalists.

Go to School to Get a Job

When a parent says to a child, "Go to school to get a job," they are advising their child to be *proletariat*—someone who sells their labor for money. An employee does not own the production.

If the child finds a high-paying job, they join the *bourgeois* and become a middle-class person, happy with material trappings such as a college education, house and car… comfortable being comfortable, keeping up with the Jones. They are happy to drive past the slums, tenements, and dwellings of the proletariat, making sure their kids do not go to school with "those kids." Most of the bourgeois have a high-paying job; many are self-employed specialists such as doctors and lawyers, or small business entrepreneurs. But they do not own the real estate or the production. These people work for money.

The Rich Do Not Work for Money

In *Rich Dad Poor Dad*, rich dad's lesson #1 is, "The rich do not work for money." When I ask, "What was rich dad's lesson #1?" most readers do not recall this lesson. I believe this is because they have been programmed to "Go to school and find a job." They have not been trained to be a person who owns the production. In other words, our educational system trains students to be *proletariat* and *bourgeois*... rather than capitalists, the people who own the land, businesses, and capital.

Small wonder we have millions of people who, like my poor dad—a highly educated man, a government bureaucrat, who sincerely believed he was helping others—are dependent upon the government to provide them with a job, paycheck, and pension. People unable, unfortunately, to help themselves.

In 1970, my dad, a very good man, ran for lieutenant governor of the State of Hawaii against his boss, the governor, a Democrat. After my father lost the election, the governor vowed my dad, a PhD in education, would never work in state government again. My dad died a poor man, unemployed... willing to work but unable to find a job. He was a highly educated man who did not own any production, a teacher who taught thousands of others to do what he did.

Small wonder we have class warfare erupting on the streets of America and around the world.

Small wonder that Senator Bernie Sanders, during his 2016 run for the U.S. presidency, stated: *"There is something profoundly wrong when the top one-tenth of one percent owns almost as much wealth as the bottom 90 percent."*

Simply put, our global financial crisis begins in our schools. The United States spends billions on teacher education, yet the gap between rich and poor grows worse.

As Karl Marx wrote:

> *"The proletarians have nothing to lose but their chains. They have a world to win. Workingmen of all countries, unite!"*

As Ayn Rand stated:

> *"He is free to evade reality… but not free to avoid the abyss he refuses to see."*

Think of that the next time you hear someone say to a child, "Go to school to get a job."

Originally written for *Jetset* magazine

Why "job security" is an obsolete idea.

Globalization took out blue-collar jobs.
Robots will take white-collar jobs.

"Income inequality has since soared to levels not seen since 1929,
and it has become clear that the productivity increases
that went into workers' pockets back in the 1950s
are now being retained almost entirely
by business owners and investors."

– Martin Ford, *Rise of the Robots*

Why "investing for the long-term in the stock market" is obsolete advice.

"Most threatening are sleeper attack viruses
planted deep in stock exchange operating systems.

"One such attack virus planted by Russian military intelligence
was discovered inside the operating system
of the NASDAQ stock market in 2010.
The virus was disabled.
No one knows how many undiscovered digital viruses
are lying in wait.

**"Viruses can erase customer accounts without trace.
Used offensively, these viruses can create an uncontrolled flood
of sell orders on widely held stocks such as Apple or Amazon."**

– James Rickards, *The Road to Ruin*

DEATH OF DEMOCRACY

"A democracy is always temporary in nature;
it simply cannot exist as a permanent form of government.
A democracy will continue to exist up
until the time that voters discover
that they can vote themselves generous gifts
from the public treasury."

"From that moment on, the majority always votes
for the candidates who promise the most benefits
from the public treasury, with the result that
every democracy will finally collapse due to loose fiscal policy,
which is always followed by a dictatorship."

The average age of the world's greatest civilizations from the beginning of history has been about 200 years. During those 200 years, these nations always progressed through the following sequence:

- From bondage to spiritual faith
- From spiritual faith to great courage
- From courage to liberty
- From liberty to abundance
- From abundance to selfishness
- From selfishness to apathy
- From apathy to dependence
- From dependency back to bondage once more.

The Cult of Competency (1943)
– Henning Webb Prentis, Jr.
President, National Association of Manufacturers

WHAT IS FINANCIAL EDUCATION... REALLY?

Obviously, financial education is a massive subject, far greater than what can be covered in any one book. And, in keeping with Rich Dad tradition, I will KISS: Keep It Super Simple.

Real financial education can be broken into two parts. They are: Financial Literacy and Financial IQ.

1: FINANCIAL LITERACY – The ability to read and understand the language of money.

In *Rich Dad Poor Dad*, two important words of money are *asset* and *liability*. As stated in the book, people get into financial trouble calling their liabilities assets. For example, they call their house an asset, and their car an asset, when they are really liabilities.

The Most Important Words of Money: Cash Flow

The most important words in the language of money are cash flow. As described in *Rich Dad Poor Dad*, assets put money in your pocket and liabilities take money from your pocket.

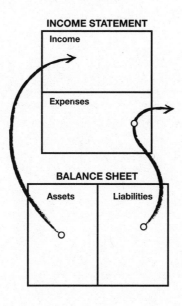

2: FINANCIAL IQ – The ability to solve financial problems.

Recently, a poll stated that the average American family cannot afford an extra $400 for an unexpected emergency. This means the average American has a Financial IQ of less than $400.

A person like President Trump has a Financial IQ, measured in dollars, in the millions. As a private citizen, if he had a $25 million unexpected expense, he could simply write a personal check. How big a check could Bernie Sanders write?

How high is your financial IQ? How big of an unexpected bill could you pay if you had to?

The Highest of Financial IQs

One reason why rich entrepreneurs are getting richer is because they have extremely high financial IQs. In this book, you will find out how very smart rich people know how to use debt (a liability to most people) to buy assets. And you will learn how those with very high financial IQs know how to use tax dollars, normally paid to the government, to buy assets for themselves.

If *Rich Dad Poor Dad* was elementary school, this book, *Why the Rich Are Getting Richer,* is graduate school.

RDTV

As a supplement to this book, RDTV offers you 10 financial education lessons. Much like Ted Talks, with RDTV you will learn how to increase your financial literacy and financial IQ—learning how the rich use debt and taxes to make them richer—just by watching TV.

All Millionaires Are Not Created Equal

Many people aspire to become millionaires. Yet, not all millionaires are equal. Some millionaires are richer than others.

The Atlantic.com reported in "Severe Inequality Is Incompatible With the American Dream," by Alana Semuels that a new study has quantified what many Millennials have experienced for years.

"The paper puts numbers on what many have seen firsthand for years: The American dream—the ability to climb the economic ladder and achieve more than one's parents did—is less and less a reality with every decade that goes by.

"People born in the 1940s had a 92 percent chance of earning more than their parents did at age 30. For people born in the 1980s, by contrast, the chances were just 50-50.

"There are two main reasons why today's 30-somethings have a harder time than their parents did, according to the authors. First, the expansion of the gross domestic product has slowed since the 1950s, when growth was frequently above 5 percent a quarter. That means the economic pie is growing at a slower rate than it once did, so there's less to go around. Second, the distribution of that growth is more unequal, and more benefits are accruing to those at the top. Those at the bottom, on the other hand, are not able to achieve as big a share as they once did. Their wages are not growing, so they are stuck at the same level as, or below, their parents.

"People at the bottom half of the income distribution are making, on average, $16,000 a year, while the average pre-tax income of the top 1 percent of adults is about $1.3 million."

In other words, a society in which most of the poor stay poor and the rich stay rich. The American Dream is dead, especially if you go to school and look for a job. A real financial education would offer a more ambitious person different avenues to become a millionaire, even in today's economy.

The Different Types of Millionaires

There are different types of millionaires. A few are:

1. **A million-dollar-a-year job.** The odds of a recent college graduate securing a job with a million-dollar paycheck in corporate America are slim to none, even if that person is a graduate of Harvard or Stanford. In most cases, it takes years to climb the ladder to the top. A person with a million-dollar salary will net approximately $600,000.

2. **A millionaire sports star.** If you are an outstanding athlete, you have a shot at earning a million-dollar salary for a few years. Sixty-five percent of all professional athletes are bankrupt five years after retirement. A million-dollar salary to a pro football player without financial education, an employee of a professional team, would net approximately $400,000.

3. **A millionaire movie star or rock star.** Again, the odds are against them. Their future is in the hands of their fans. Without financial education, a million dollars to a rock star would also net around $300,000 to $400,000 after taxes.

4. **A millionaire entrepreneur.** Same odds. Many small business owners earn less than their employees when total time and compensation are calculated. Without a financial education, a million dollars will net a small business entrepreneur approximately $300,000.

Financial Education

A real financial education levels the playing field. The road is still rough, and earning a million dollars is not easy. But a real financial education offers everyone greater control over their financial future. In other words, a real financial education puts your financial future in your hands.

I am that person. There was little chance of me earning a million-dollar salary as a CEO, climbing the corporate ladder to success, or becoming a major sports star, movie star, singer, or famous entrepreneur. Yet, with my rich dad's financial education, I was able to take control over my financial destiny.

When I was a young boy, my rich dad encouraged me to go for my dreams and become a millionaire. He also explained there are different types of millionaires and different ways to become a millionaire.

1. *Do you want to be an employee with a million-dollar salary?* The problem with a million-dollar salary is taxes, approximately 40% going to the government.

2. *Do you want to be a net worth millionaire?* That means you have taken the value of all your personal assets—your house, car, savings, and pension—and subtracted liabilities from those assets. Most people who claim to be millionaires are net worth millionaires. Many net worth millionaires have salaries of less than $150,000 a year.

3. *Do you want to be a capital gains millionaire?* That means, you sell assets for a million dollars in capital gains which are subject to capital gains taxes. A big problem for capital gains millions is taxes. Capital gains taxes are approximately 10% to 20% on capital gains income. The bigger problem is that a capital gains millionaire reduces his or her net worth because they must sell assets for money.

4. *Do you want to be a cash flow millionaire?* These are people who have a million dollars or more coming in as cash flow from assets *without* selling their assets. Cash flow millionaires have the most control over taxes and their future.

5. *Do you want to be a lucky millionaire by marrying a rich person, inheriting money, or winning the lottery?* To you I say, "Good luck." The price of marrying for money can be your soul. How much is your soul worth?

The American Dream Is Dead

The American Dream is dead for most people; especially people who believe in going to school, getting a job, saving money, and investing for the long-term in a retirement plan.

Yet the dream of becoming a millionaire is alive and well, if a person invests in a real financial education, which this book is about.

When I was a young boy, playing *Monopoly*® with rich dad, I knew I wanted to become a cash flow millionaire. I knew that four green houses led to one red hotel, which increased my cash flow and my net worth. Being a cash flow millionaire allows me to use debt as money, pay less in taxes, legally, without selling assets, which would decrease my net worth.

What do you want to do? What kind of millionaire do you want to be?

CONTENTS

A MESSAGE FROM ROBERT

Why Tom Wheelwright?

If you are an employee, you probably don't need a CPA. There is little that a CPA can do for employees, or their taxes. There are smart CPAs and stupid CPAs; courageous CPAs and gutless ones. Tom is both courageous and smart. If you want to be rich, you must have a CPA who's as smart as Tom.

Tom Wheelwright began his career in accounting as a young man working as the accounts payable clerk at his father's printing business. After high school, Tom served a mission for the Mormon Church in Paris, France, learning leadership skills as well as handling the accounting for 175 missionaries in northern France for nine months as the financial secretary to the mission president.

After his mission, Tom attended the University of Utah, graduating with a Bachelor of Arts degree with a major in accounting and a minor in French. He worked for two different accounting firms, doing bookkeeping for one and tax return preparation for the other. Tom attended the University of Texas at Austin receiving his Masters of Professional Accounting degree with a specialty in Taxation. He also worked for a local CPA firm preparing taxes while attending the University of Texas.

After graduating from Texas, Tom began his career at Ernst & Whinney, one of the Big Eight accounting firms, in Salt Lake City Utah. After two years, he was invited to join the National Tax Department in Washington, D.C. He served for three years in National Tax, creating and teaching courses to the firm's thousands of CPAs throughout the United States and handling complex tax issues for the firm's entrepreneurial, real estate, and oil and gas clientele.

Tom rotated out of National Tax to the Phoenix office where he was in charge of the real estate tax practice for that office. Two years later, he joined Pinnacle West Capital Corporation, then a Fortune 500 company, as in-house tax advisor. Four years later, Tom joined Price Waterhouse, another international CPA firm, as director of state and local tax services for the Phoenix office.

After a short time at Price Waterhouse, Tom decided to open his own CPA firm. He started with two clients and within five years his firm was one of the top 50 CPA firms in Phoenix. Since then, Tom's firm, ProVision, has grown to one of the top 20 CPA firms in Arizona, handling complex tax matters for clients in all 50 states and in over 30 countries on six continents. Tom has created innovative tax strategies to routinely reduce taxes for ProVision's clients by 10-40% or more. Tom is an accomplished speaker who writes for *The Tax Adviser, The Journal of Partnership Taxation,* and *Accounting Today.* He is the author of the best-selling book *Tax-Free Wealth.*

PREFACE

Why Crashes Made Robert and Kim Richer

I first met Robert and Kim Kiyosaki in January 2002. The prior month, my partner, Ann, and I had acquired an accounting firm that included them as clients. I didn't know much about them at the time. My friend, George, had sent me a notification in early November 2001 that he had just joined The Rich Dad Company as its Chief Financial Officer. And another friend, Kim, was also a client of the accounting firm we had acquired and gave me some insight into the Kiyosakis.

But it wasn't until I really got to know Robert and Kim over the years that I began to understand their genius. This was not an ordinary couple who had written a best-selling book. This was a most unusual couple who practiced everything they taught. They didn't teach from a book. They taught from their life's lessons. They had truly learned why the rich get richer and how to join the ranks of the rich and famous without losing their way or their sense of who they are.

The magic of Robert and Kim Kiyosaki is not that they know something nobody else knows or that they are the only people who have become rich and famous teaching people how to make money. The magic of Robert and Kim is that they are true examples of what they teach. Everything in this book is based on how they live their lives. I know this because I have been their CPA for the past 15 years. I have watched them make money, and I have watched them lose money. I have never seen them do something they don't believe—or teach something they haven't done.

This authenticity, this trueness to their being, is what most attracts me, and so many others, to the Kiyosaki brand. I have traveled throughout the world with them. We have been together in Europe, Asia, Africa, Australia, South America, across the United States and

Canada. We have spoken to audiences in Estonia, Poland, Moscow, Kiev, Sydney, Melbourne, Johannesburg, Almaty, Bishkek, Helsinki, London, Tokyo and Shanghai. I have watched as they graciously speak to every person who stops them on the street for a picture or an autograph. I remember a young man at border control in Kiev asking Robert for an autograph and receiving not just an autograph, but a selfie with Robert as well. I remember the woman in Moscow stopping Robert on the street and telling him that she would be at his event in Rome and his sincere interest as he listened to her story.

This book is the culmination of Robert and Kim's story. It is truly a success story that few people have ever matched. What makes it magical is the simplicity of this story. Robert was taught some basic principals of finance that he and Kim practiced diligently and with great success. It is a story of buying low and selling high. It's a story of education and being prepared for when the markets crashed. It's a story of persistence in the face of great opposition and dedication to a truth nobody else was willing to discuss.

Robert and Kim's story began the day they went on their first date. Robert asked Kim what she wanted out of life. She was a little taken aback by such a deep question on a first date. Still, she answered very thoughtfully that she wanted her own business. She didn't want to be an employee, as she had tried that route without success. She thought she would do much better as an entrepreneur. She had no idea at the time just how prophetic this decision would turn out to be.

Then, on their first anniversary (or was it her birthday?), Robert gave Kim a most unusual gift. He didn't give her a diamond or a bracelet. He had enrolled her into an accounting course. Robert believed that if Kim were to succeed in her business, she had better learn accounting. (How I wish more of my clients would give their spouse an accounting course for a gift!)

Robert and Kim went on a journey of learning about money. Robert had learned much from his friend's father, whom he calls his

Rich Dad. And he learned more from his mentor, R. Buckminster Fuller. He learned the most, however, from the school of hard knocks. His first business, a surfer wallet business, was successful quickly—and, just as quickly, turned into a failure. His second business, t-shirts and baseball caps for rock-star events, was an even bigger success and an even bigger failure, putting Robert in the hole for over $800,000 by the time he met Kim. So we know Kim didn't marry Robert for his money.

My experience is that all entrepreneurs who have had great success have also had great failures. Steve Jobs failed, getting fired from his own company. Donald Trump was at one time $800 million in debt with no clear path for digging his way out. The experience of failure gave these entrepreneurs education and experience and the strength to carry on.

For Robert and Kim, experience and education was priceless. By the time the first big crash of the late 20th century occurred in 1989 and 1990, they were ready. They had studied real estate and accounting and they had learned the lessons of business. So when the Savings and Loans in the United States went belly up, they were ready to take action.

And that they did. They bought up real estate for pennies on the dollar. Within a few years, their income from real estate far exceeded their expenses. Nobody would have called them rich, but they were financially free. They had passive income of about $10,000 per month and their expenses were only about $3,000 per month. They decided that this was something they should teach others how to do.

So, from their little house in Bisbee, Arizona, they created a game to teach the lessons they had learned about money. They called it *CASHFLOW 101*. In order to sell the game, they knew they had to develop a brochure. Robert's task was to write the brochure. As he was writing down the principals he had learned from both his rich dad and through life's lessons, he found he couldn't keep it to an 8-page brochure. So it became a 132-page book… that he titled *Rich Dad Poor Dad*.

The release of *Rich Dad Poor Dad* was the second time Robert and Kim capitalized on a crash. The book was released in 1997. Nobody would publish the book, so Robert and Kim self-published it. The book hit it big when network marketers adopted it as a tool to promote home-based businesses. But it wasn't until Oprah Winfrey invited Robert to be a guest on her show in April of 2000 that it really took off.

This was right after the dot-com crash so the timing was perfect. *Rich Dad Poor Dad* stayed at the top of *The New York Times* Bestsellers list for more than six years. Robert and Kim had stuck a chord with the public, both in the United States and around the world. As millions were losing their life savings, Robert and Kim were giving them an alternative to the financial markets, an alternative that included taking control of their life, their money, and their future.

Robert and Kim could have sat on the sidelines and collected royalties from *Rich Dad Poor Dad*. They couldn't do that, though, as it would have violated their core principles and their mission of increasing the financial literacy of the world. So they wrote more books, taught more seminars, and gave more interviews… generously sharing all that they had learned.

In 2002, Robert wrote *Rich Dad's Prophecy*. In it, he predicted a major crash by 2016 and a smaller crash ahead of that one. In 2005, he was seen on CNN predicting the upcoming real estate crash. Then, in 2008 and 2009, both the real estate and the stock markets took a nosedive, just as Robert had predicted.

Robert could have called CNN and said, "I told you so." Instead, he and Kim got busy taking advantage of the crash just the way they had taught millions of others to do. They bought millions of dollars of real estate when the market was low. Today they own thousands of properties, including apartments, hotels, and golf courses. All because they practiced what they preached and they were ready for the crash, ready for opportunities that came their way.

This book is all about crashes—how to get ready for them, how to identify them, and how to benefit from them. Nobody wants a market to crash, as crashes are devastating to the poor and uneducated. But nobody can prevent a crash, either. Crashes come because governments prop up markets. They come from events outside of any one person's control. Not even a president can prevent a crash.

Your response to the coming crash, including your preparation for it, will in large part determine your financial future for years to come. It's your choice. Will you prepare yourself with the financial education you'll find in this book? Will you be ready to take the actions required to profit from the coming crash? Only those who do will be safe from the effects of the crash. Most people will be devastated by the crash. A few will become multi-millionaires. Which will you be?

– Tom Wheelwright, CPA and Rich Dad Advisor
and best-selling author of *Tax-Free Wealth*
Founder of ProVision PLC

INTRODUCTION

ONCE UPON A TIME… *all a person had to do was go to school, get a job, work hard, save money, buy a house, get out of debt, invest for the long term in the stock market, and live happily ever after.*

That fairytale is over.

One of the primary reasons for the growing gap between the rich, poor, and middle class is this fairytale. Simply put, the people following this fairytale are falling into the chasm between rich and poor. People who still believe in this fairytale are in financial trouble today.

Twenty Years Ago

In 1997, *Rich Dad Poor Dad* was first published. It was self-published because not one of the publishers we contacted thought I knew what I was talking about. And, I believe, most of my rich dad's lessons did not make sense 20 years ago. Twenty years ago, *Rich Dad Poor Dad* was written as a warning of the coming economic crisis we are in today. And, 20 years ago, I was lambasted for saying that "your house is not an asset" and "savers are losers." But times have changed.

You may recall, 20 years ago, in 1997, the stock market was booming, jobs were plentiful, and the most popular book was *The Millionaire Next Door*, published in 1996. *The Millionaire Next Door* was a story about the people who followed the fairytale—*"go to school, get a job, save money, get out of debt, and live happily ever after."* Simply put, in 1996, it was easy to get rich; almost everyone was getting rich.

The millionaire next door had a college education, a good job, drove a conservative car, owned a house that was going up in value, and money in the stock market via a pension plan or a personal retirement plan. Life was good. It was easy to become a millionaire. The American Dream was a reality.

A Warning

In 1996, Federal Reserve Bank Chairman, Alan Greenspan warned of "irrational exuberance," which meant people were drunk and delirious, believing getting rich was easy.

In 1997, *Rich Dad Poor Dad* was released. *Rich Dad Poor Dad* was on the opposite side of the coin from *The Millionaire Next Door.* My rich dad did not believe in job security, saving money, living below your means, driving an economy car, getting out of debt, or investing for the long term in the stock market.

The World Changed

Then, in 2000, the dot-com bubble burst, 9/11 drove home the fact that global terrorism was *not* that far from our doors, the real estate bubble bust in 2007, and the nation's biggest banks crashed in 2008. Interest rates were cut to below zero and savers became losers. Oil prices plunged causing oil-based economies to wobble; and the War on Terror escalated. The European Union came under strain as Greece, Italy, and Spain struggled. The rich got richer as the stock market reached new heights... but the working poor and middle class got poorer. Today, the world is tossing and turning through the toughest economic crisis in history.

Twenty Years Later

Today, many millionaires next door are unemployed and their house is the "foreclosure next door."

Today, young people are going to school, graduating (burdened, in many cases, with crushing student loan debt), and often unable to find that mythical high-paying job. Today, U.S. student loan debt is $1.2 trillion, greater than U.S. credit card debt.

Many students will never be able to afford a house because they do not earn enough money and are paying off their student loans. Many students—and college graduates—still live at home.

Many educated young people have found jobs, but are underemployed. The failure of young people to gain priceless, meaningful, challenging, real-life work and business experience is another time bomb for our future.

Savers Are Losers

Today savers are losers. Interest rates on savings are at historic lows. Japan, Sweden, and the Eurozone have negative interest rates.

Pensions Are in Trouble

Most pension plans, private and public, operate on a 7.5% return on pensioner's savings. CalPERS,

California Public Employees' Retirement System—and the biggest government employee pension plan in the United States—is operating at less than a 2% return on equity, which means millions of government employees' pensions are underwater.

Social Security and Medicare are in the red. Is another massive taxpayer bailout on horizon?

The Robots Are Coming

Making matters worse, the robots are coming. In his book, *Rise of the Robots: Technology and the Threat of a Jobless Future,* Martin Ford explains why the fairytale of going to school to get a secure job is delusional. Odds are that, even if you are a medical doctor, a robot can replace you… *today*, not tomorrow.

The world's richest countries are racing to develop robots, technology, to replace human beings. Not only may McDonald's employees soon be out of work, but the future of journalists, teachers, and professionals like lawyers, doctors, and accountants are also problematic. Martin Ford was not writing about jobs going overseas to low-wage countries. He is writing about humans being replaced by robots. He states that America can now compete with low-wage countries in manufacturing. Unfortunately, America will compete with robots, not human labor. The message is clear: Mass unemployment has arrived.

Our New President

In 2016, Donald Trump was elected president of the United States in a landslide. Millions are afraid of him and what he will do. On the flip side, millions voted for him because they know the pain of cities dying and unemployment rising. I voted for him because he represented change. And, in my opinion, many things need to change.

Donald Trump is a friend of mine. We have written two books together. While I cringed at some of his off-the-cuff, insensitive remarks about women, race, and religion, the person I got to know is a good man, as well as a great parent and a great leader.

His three older children are fantastic young people. Kim and I have been invited to their weddings. His staff is made up of powerful, self-determined, articulate women who have been with him for decades. His wife Melania is elegant, beautiful, and speaks her mind—as well as five languages. My wife Kim respects Donald Trump because of the way he treats women.

Donald Trump and I got together to write books because we are both concerned about the first line in the fairytale: "go to school." We chose to co-author books because we are both educators, we both had rich dads, and we are concerned about the quality of education in America today. We believe real financial education must be made available to all students.

President Trump has a tough job ahead because the United States and the world are in financial trouble. He, too, knows the fairy tale is over.

Why This Book?

This book is written as the graduate school version of *Rich Dad Poor Dad.* This book explains what real financial education is and why the rich are getting richer. The difference between rich, poor, and middle class is education; unfortunately not the education found in schools.

Real financial education must include a bit of financial history. This crisis did not just happen. This financial crisis has been brewing for over 100 years, since 1913, the year the Federal Reserve System and the U.S. tax system was created. This book will go into a brief history of this crisis. When you understand the historical events that have led to this crisis, you will understand why *The Millionaire Next Door,* the person who continues to believe in the fairytale, is in financial trouble today. The millionaire next door is very much like my poor dad.

For years, no one cared that factories were moving out of the country. For years, no one cared that once high-paying jobs were leaving the country. For years no one cared that towns across the United States were dying. For years, the financial, political, and academic elite lived well, out of touch with the parts of America that were dying. Senator Bernie Sanders got it, which is why he almost beat Hilary Clinton in the Democratic primary. Donald Trump gets it, which is why, today, he is the president of the United States.

Who Will Save You?

My concern is that too many people are counting on President Trump to save them. While Donald Trump is a great man, he is not Superman. I doubt he can save anyone, unless they are first willing to save themselves.

Donald Trump and I got together because we do not believe in *giving people fish*, as Bernie Sanders and many others believe. Donald Trump and I believe in *teaching people to fish*. My first book, *Rich Dad Poor Dad* was written 20 years ago, in 1997, to teach people to fish.

Warning #1: Real Education

This book, *Why the Rich Are Getting Richer*, is the advanced version of *Rich Dad Poor Dad*—Rich Dad Graduate School. If you have not read *Rich Dad Poor Dad*, I suggest you read that book first, before reading this book. This book is for graduate students of Rich Dad, those already familiar with the principles and lessons in that book. As with all rich dad books, I have done my best to keep things simple. This book is simple, but what the rich do is not easy.

The 90/10 Rule of Money

There is a rule of money known as the 90/10 Rule. That rule states that 10% of the people earn 90% of the money. This book and *Rich Dad Poor Dad* are about the 90/10 rule of money.

The good news is that with *real* financial education, almost everyone can be in the 10% who earn 90% of money. In this book, you will find out why it does not require a high-priced college education from a prestigious school to be part of the 10%. In fact, many of the richest people in the world, never finished college: Steve Jobs, Mark Zuckerberg, and Walt Disney being among them.

The challenge for you is to decide. Do you have the spirit, determination, and drive to gain a real financial education? If you are a quitter, don't want to work hard, or are not willing to study, this book is not for you.

If you are a person who believes that life should be easy and the government should take care of you, then *this book is definitely not for you.*

The point is, this book is about real financial education, the education not found in school.

Warning #2: Taxes

President Barack Obama beat Republican candidate Governor Mitt Romney in 2012 for many reasons. One reason was taxes. Barack Obama disclosed that he paid 30% in taxes. Mitt Romney paid less than 14% in taxes on income of over $20 million.

Donald Trump never released his tax returns, which drove his opponents crazy. Whether that was smart or devious depends upon your point of view on taxes.

Much of this book is about taxes. If you love paying taxes and want to pay more in taxes, this book is not for you. If you want to learn how people like Mitt Romney and Donald Trump make millions and pay very little in taxes, this book is for you.

Taxes Are Fair

Many people believe taxes are unfair. What is unfair is the lack of real financial education that would help people to better *understand* taxes. The fact is that tax laws are for everyone. Anyone can pay less in taxes… if they have real financial education to use the tax law to their advantage.

Since taxes are such a hot and controversial subject, I have asked my personal tax advisor, Tom Wheelwright, to be my adjuvant, my authority on the subject of taxes in writing this book. Tom is the smartest, brightest, most diligent CPA I have ever met. One reason the rich get richer is because they have advisors like Tom guiding them.

The challenge is that an advisor like Tom Wheelwright can only do so much. If you truly want to earn millions and pay less, even zero, in taxes, you have to do what the rich do. Tom can do very little to help the millionaire next door.

Tax Lessons from Tom

Taxes Reward the Financially Educated

Taxes are not intended to punish people. They are intended to reward those who do what the government wants them to do. It takes financial education and action to know and to do what the government will reward you to do. This book will give you insights into how the government rewards those willing to follow their policies. For more in-depth information on the tax rewards for being financially educated I invite you to take a look at my Rich Dad Advisor series book *Tax-Free Wealth* or visit TaxFreeWealthAdvisor.com.

Warning #3: You Can't Do This

"You can't do this here." Tom Wheelwright and the other Rich Dad Advisors travel the world teaching the lessons taught in this book.

Everywhere we visit, including cities across the United States, there are people who raise their hands and say, "You can't do that here." In most instances, the person is like the millionaire next door, often a medical doctor, lawyer, accountant, or financial advisor.

As you read this book, you too will probably say, "You can't do this here." The reason most people say they "can't" is because they lack real financial education.

Tom Wheelwright often invites another CPA, from the country we are visiting, to join us on stage to verify that what we teach *can* be done in the country we are in. Even then, people will argue: "You can't do this here."

And the fact is *they* can't. Without the real financial education described in this book, no one can do what the rich do, even if they are medical doctors, MBAs, lawyers, or even other CPAs.

The following diagram explains who cannot do what we do.

People who say "You can't do this here" are most often Es, employees, and Ss, *small business owners*, or *specialists*, such as doctors or lawyers, or the *self-employed*, people like real estate agents, web designers, and hairdressers.

Looking at this diagram again, you may get a better idea of why some people say "You can't do this here"… and why some people are doing it.

The B quadrant stands for big business, businesses with 500 employees or more.

The I quadrant represents professional investors.

Most Es and Ss invest like the millionaire next door. They are retail investors who invest in stocks, bonds, mutual funds, and ETFs. Professional investors are people who manufacture their own investments or invest at wholesale prices. The people who say, "You can't do this" are Es and Ss who invest in paper assets.

This book describes what people in the B and I quadrants really know and do. You can do what the B and I quadrants do, if you are willing to invest in your real financial education. If you do, you will be one of the few who truly know why the rich are getting richer.

Joining the 90/10 Club

If you are willing to do what it takes to make it to the B and I quadrants, you will join the 90/10 Club, in that 10 percent that makes 90 percent of the money.

If you are not willing to join the ranks of the 10%, you can join the crowd who would rather say "You can't do this here"… even if they could.

The reason most people say, "You can't do this here" is because it is easier to push back and challenge the prospect of actually *doing* it… than to do it. This book is for anyone, rich or poor, highly educated or not, who wants to do it.

Robert is not a Republican or Democrat.
He is an Independent voter and an advocate for financial education.

The mission of The Rich Dad Company:
to elevate the financial well-being of humanity

Part One

WHY THE RICH ARE GETTING RICHER

Introduction to Part One

THE OTHER SIDE
OF THE COIN

All coins have three sides: heads, tails, and the edge.

Intelligence is found on the edge of the coin, and in the ability to see both sides.

Part One of this book focuses on the side of the coin of the rich.

In Part One, you will discover how *taxes* make the poor and middle class poorer, yet on the other side, the very same tax laws make the rich richer.

The same is true for *debt*. Debt makes the poor and middle class poorer, while debt makes the rich richer.

After reading Part One, you will be better able to stand on the edge of the coin, appreciate both points of view and decide which side is best for you.

Chapter One

WHAT SHOULD I DO WITH MY MONEY?

Poor Dad:

"I'm not interested in money."

Rich Dad:

*"If you are not interested in your money,
someone else is."*

A question I am often asked is:

"I have $10,000. What should I do with my money?"

I've lost track of how many people, in cities around the world, have asked me that question. Everyone is looking for that magic pill, the easy answer. And although the amount of money may vary—ranging from $1,000 to $2.5 million—the question I'm asked is always the same. *What should I do with my money?*

My standard reply is:

"Please do not announce to the world that you are 'clueless with money.' If you do not know what to do with your money, there are millions of people who will tell you what to do. In many cases what they'll tell you is, 'Give your money to me.'"

The Small Picture

What you do with your money is the *small picture*—the final step—the last piece of your financial puzzle.

This book is about the *big picture*—an attempt to look at the whole picture, the entire puzzle. Then you can decide which pieces of the puzzle are best for you.

As rich dad often said:

"There are many doors to financial heaven."

The Middle Class and the Poor... Get Poorer

The world is printing money. Our money is toxic. Our money is unstable causing instability in the world economy. The more toxic money that is created, the wider the gap between the rich, poor, and middle class.

Another reason the rich are getting richer is because the poor and middle class focus on the small picture. Most people have been taught to *work hard, pay taxes, save money, buy a house, get out of debt, and invest in the stock market.*

These are small picture action steps. These are the same steps most parents, teachers, and financial experts tell you to follow.

Words from Warren

Warren Buffett, one of the richest men in the world and arguably one of the world's smartest investors, has this to say about financial advisors:

"Wall Street is the only place that people ride to in a Rolls Royce to get advice from those who take the subway."

Rich dad said it this way: *"The reason the middle class struggle financially is because they take advice from salespeople, not rich people."*

A sales person must sell to put food on the table. They need money. If they do not sell, they do not eat. That is why it is foolish to announce to the world, *"I have $10,000 and I am a financial idiot. Tell me what to do."*

Warren Buffett said:

> *"Never ask an insurance salesman if you need more insurance. The answer is always 'Yes.'"*

Buffett should know. He owns one of the largest auto insurance companies in America, GEICO. He is a very rich man who hires salespeople to sell for him.

Ask most financial salespeople how much financial education they have. The honest answer is "not much."

Ask how many books on money they have read, and the answer is probably the same. Not many.

Then ask them if they are rich. Ask them if they can stop working and still put food on the table?

Man vs. Monkey

Years ago there was a contest between a monkey and professional stock pickers.

The monkey picked stocks by throwing darts at a dartboard, with names of companies as targets.

The stock pickers used their education, training, and intellectual skills to analyze company values before choosing a stock.

The monkey won.

High-Paid Losers

March 12, 2015, *CNN Money* ran an article stating:

> *"A staggering 86% of active large-cap fund managers failed to beat their benchmarks."*

The highly-educated, high-paid experts could not beat the market. The article goes on to say,

> *"And no, that wasn't a one-off blip either. Nearly 89% of those fund managers underperformed their benchmarks over the past five years and 82% did the same over the last decade,' S&P said."*

In other words, if a monkey had simply picked the S&P 500 Index fund, the monkey would have beat 90% of the experts over five years and 80% of the experts over 10 years. The lesson here is that if a monkey can beat the high-paid experts... so can you.

The S&P 500

Just because a monkey can beat the S&P 500, does not mean the S&P is making money. The monkey and the S&P lose money. As you can see from the chart below the S&P also had its ups and downs.

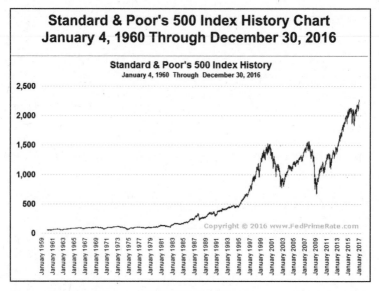

Source: FedPrimeRate.com | S&P 500 Index History

So, why invest for the long term? Why lose money when markets crash? Diversification won't protect you from losing money. The S&P is an extremely diversified group of 500 stocks.

Warren Buffett

Even Warren Buffett's company, Berkshire Hathaway, did not do much better than the S&P 500 after the crashes began in 2000.

Berkshire Hathaway vs. S&P 500 (5-Year Return)

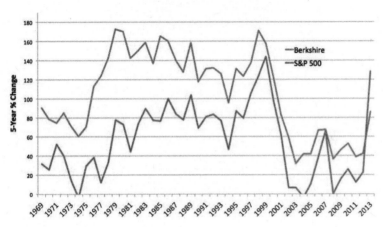

Source: Business Insider

I wonder what will happen when the next crash arrives.

Q: *Are you saying Warren Buffet did not beat the S&P 500? Are you saying he lost money too?*

A: Just look at the chart.

Q: *So who invests with him?*

A: People who ask the question: "What should I do with my money?"

Q: *What about the people who lose money? Don't you feel badly for them?*

A: Absolutely. Why do you think I teach, write books, and create financial games? I've been broke. I've lost money, so I know how it feels. It breaks my heart to witness people struggling financially.

If Warren Buffett can lose money, don't you think you should consider investing in your financial education before you turn your money over to the experts?

After all, if a monkey can beat the experts, why can't you?

Chapter Two

WHY SAVERS ARE LOSERS

Poor Dad:

"Saving money is smart."

Rich Dad:

"Savers are losers."

August 15, 1971 was ***the official start*** of today's financial crisis.

August 15, 1971 was the day President Richard Nixon ***took the dollar off the gold standard.***

It's the Money, Stupid

August 15, 1971 was the date the ***United States began printing money.***

August 15, 1971 was **the official date the rich began getting richer**—and the poor and middle class began getting poorer.

August 15, 1971 was the day **savers became losers**.

The Warning

On April 8, 1997, *Rich Dad Poor Dad* was officially launched. The book was self-published because every publisher we took the book to turned it down, a few commenting, *"You do not know what you are talking about."*

The publishers did not agree with many of my rich dad's lessons on money, especially, rich dad's lesson #1:

"The rich do not work for money."

Rich Dad's Lesson #1 is the cornerstone of rich dad's financial education.

There are many reasons why the rich do not work for money. One reason is taxes. Rich dad often said, *"The people who work for money pay the highest percentage in taxes."*

The primary reason is because after 1971, the U.S. dollar stopped being money. It became a fiat currency.

Q: *What is a fiat currency?*

A: A fiat currency is valueless money, and not backed by anything of value except by *government decree.*

Q: *What is a government decree?*

A: Simply put, the government creates laws, saying that a piece of paper is money, legal tender. For example, people must pay their taxes in a country's fiat currency. You cannot pay your taxes in gold or in chickens.

Q: *What's wrong with fiat currency?*

A: Governments tend to spend more than they collect in taxes. They make promises they cannot always keep. So they print fiat currency to pay their bills, making that fiat currency worth less and less.

Q: *So I have to work harder... and life gets more expensive?*

A: Exactly.

Q: *Have fiat currencies become worthless?*

A: Eventually they all become worthless because government bureaucrats do not know how to make money. They only know how to spend money.

The French philosopher Voltaire (1694-1778) said:

"Paper money eventually returns to its intrinsic value—zero."

As long as the U.S. dollar was backed by gold, it was difficult to print money. Once the U.S. dollar was no longer backed by gold, the printing presses began printing and savers became losers.

Money Is Toxic

After 1971, the U.S. dollar became toxic. In 1971, the U.S. dollar became debt—an IOU from American taxpayers. As long as the taxpayer did not complain, the presses kept running. Printing toxic money was like giving alcohol to a drunken sailor. Alcohol makes an alcoholic feel good and so does money, even if it's toxic money.

For 29 years, from 1971 to 2000, the world partied on. Unfortunately, the party is over.

The 30-Year Party

The chart below tells the story of the 30-year party.

120 Years of the Dow

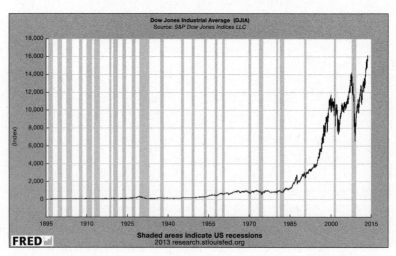

Source: FRED–Federal Reserve Economic Data

As you can see from the chart above, the party began to wind down around year 2000, the start of the 21ˢᵗ century.

Three Giant Crashes

In the first 10 years of this century, the world has gone through three giant crashes.

First, the dot-com crash in 2000, then the real estate crash in 2007, followed by the stock market crash in 2008.

Each time the markets crashed, the printing presses were kicked into gear, printing more money, hoping the economy would not collapse.

Q: *So the boom between 1971 and 2000 was created by printed money?*

A: Yes.

Q: *But now the party is over?*

A: Yes.

Q: *And they are still printing money? Hoping more printed money will save the economy?*

A: Yes. And this is why savers are losers.

Today, interest rates for savings are near or below zero. Once again, savers are losers.

Ironically, the banks today have too much money. Yet people are getting poorer. The reason for this is that our money is toxic. *Money* is making people poorer. People who work for money and save money are getting sick.

Why Savers Are Losers

In 1976, a person could save money and become rich.

For example:

In 1976, $1 million in savings X 15% interest = $150,0000 annually. You could live well on $150,000 a year in 1976.

Things are very different today.

Today, $1 million in savings X 2% interest = $20,000 annually. That is how much the value of money has gone down.

And 2% interest is high today.

Let's look at interest rates relative to inflation. If inflation is at 5%, you're looking at losing 3% on your money per year. There is inflation because governments continue to print money.

Add this fact to the mix: In **30% of the world,** interest rates are below zero.

Q: *The banks will charge me to keep my money?*

A: That is what negative interest rates mean.

Q: *Why would anyone save money if the bank is charging me money to save my money?*

A: I do not know. It makes no sense to me.

One reason why the rich are getting richer is because the rich love debt. The rich know how to use debt to get richer.

Low interest rates are saying to me, "Please come borrow money. Money is on sale."

Rich Dad's Prophecy

In 2002, *Rich Dad's Prophecy* was published. Rich dad predicted that the biggest crash in world history was coming in 2016, plus or minus a few years.

He also predicted that there would be several large crashes before the biggest crash of all, which he targeted for around 2016.

Q: *And those crashes came in 2000, 2007, and 2008?*

A: Yes.

Q: *How was he able to be so accurate in his predictions?*

A: There are many reasons. The main reason is that this is not the first time governments have printed money to pay their bills.

Lessons from History

The Chinese were the first to print money.

The first widespread use of paper money was in China, during the Tang Dynasty (618-907 AD). The use of paper money spread to India, Persia, and Japan, but its spread was short-lived because trade stopped when people stopped accepting paper money.

Q: *Why did people stop accepting the first paper money?*

A: Because governments always print too much money. Governments are doing the same thing today.

The Roman Empire collapsed, in part, because it began taxing the farmers to pay for their wars. When tax collections could not cover the expenses of war, the Roman emperors debased their coins. Debasing coins was their way of printing money.

Q: *What does debasing mean?*

A: It means they took precious metals such as gold and silver and mixed them with base metals like nickel and copper, devaluing their coins. Soon people did not trust the value of their coins.

The United States did the same thing in 1964, which is why our "silver" coins have a copper tinge on the edge.

The U.S. Prints Money

George Washington printed Continentals to pay for the Revolutionary War. Soldiers stopped fighting when the value of the Continental went to zero. Today, the saying "Not worth a Continental" lives on.

During the Civil War, the South printed money to fight the North. The Confederate dollar was soon worthless.

Q: *So rich dad based his prophecy on history?*

A: Yes, and on other factors. Real financial education must include financial history. History allows you to see into the future.

As New York Yankee great Yogi Berra once said:

"It's déjà vu all over again."

Today, our money grows more and more toxic as governments around the world print money.

Q: *Why are they printing money?*

A: To keep their economies from collapsing.

Look again at the 120-year chart of the Dow.

120 Years of the Dow

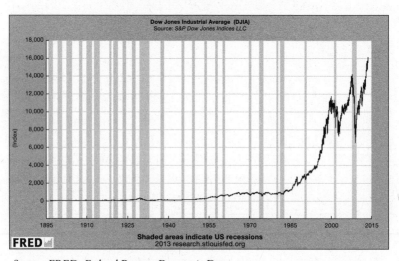

Source: FRED–Federal Reserve Economic Data

You can see that, after 1971—the year Nixon took the dollar off the gold standard—the economy took off.

Printed money blew the United States and the world into a bubble.

In 2000 the bubble started to leak. To prevent a crash, the government printed more money.

The bubble began to burst again in 2007, with the real estate crash and then, in 2008, the banks crashed. All the while the printing presses kept running.

Q: *And now the global economy may collapse?*

A: Yes. After 2008, the U.S. Federal Reserve Bank along with the U.S Treasury began the biggest printing of money in world history, an event known as *quantitative easing*.

This is what happens to fiat currency when governments print money.

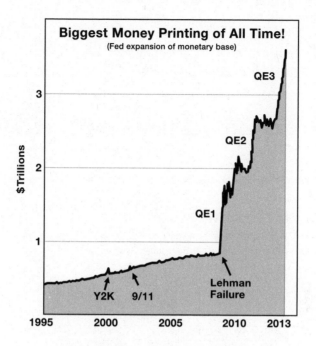

Source: MarketWatch

The U.S. dollar lost nearly 90% of its value between 1913, the year the Federal Reserve Bank was created, and 1971, the year Nixon took the dollar off the gold standard.

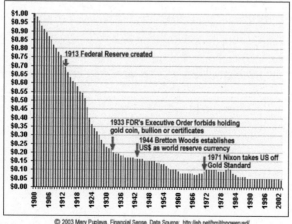

Source: Financial Sense

Between 1971 and 2016 the dollar has lost another 90% of its value.

Q: *So our money is the real reason the rich get richer, while the poor and middle class get poorer?*

A: Yes. There are four main reasons for the gap. They are:

1. **Globalization:** Jobs move to lower wage countries. Since the rich own the factories, they get richer when they can hire lower-wage employees.

Where The Jobs Are Going

U.S.-based multinational companies added jobs overseas during the 2000s and cut them at home. Cumulative change since 1999

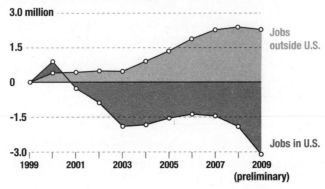

Source: Wall Street Journal

2. **Technology:** If a person who works for money wants more money, an enterprising engineer will create a robot, or software, or AI (Artificial Intelligence) to replace the worker. Robots do not need benefits or time off and will work 24/7.

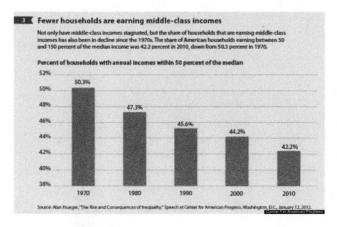

Fewer households are earning middle-class incomes

Not only have middle-class incomes stagnated, but the share of households that are earning middle-class incomes has also been in decline since the 1970s. The share of American households earning between 50 and 150 percent of the median income was 42.2 percent in 2010, down from 50.3 percent in 1970.

Percent of households with annual incomes within 50 percent of the median

Source: Alan Krueger, "The Rise and Consequences of Inequality," Speech at Center for American Progress, Washington, D.C., January 12, 2012.

Source: Alan Krueger

3. Financialization: the science of printing money.

Here are a few definitions that might be helpful:

Financialization is a process whereby financial markets, financial institutions, and financial elites gain greater influence over economic policy and economic outcomes. Financilization is the process by which financial institutions, markets, etc., increase in size and influence.

Financialization is commonly known as financial engineering.

The brightest financial engineers are building Frankenstein Monsters—monsters are known as *derivatives*. One of Dr. Frankenstein's monsters was sub-prime mortgages, sold to people who could not afford "The American Dream." These financial engineers reengineered these toxic mortgages, had them rated as *prime*, and sold them to the world as "assets."

Warren Buffett has called derivatives *"Financial weapons of mass destruction."* He should know how lethal they are. Moody's, blessed these toxic assets as *prime*.

In 2007, these weapons of mass destruction started to go off. The global economy nearly collapsed. The taxpayers bailed out the bankers who were paid bonuses rather than carted off to jail.

4. **Kleptocracy:** Crony capitalism.

You may remember this cartoon from the opening pages of this book...

There are several definitions of a kleptocracy:

1) *A government or state in which those in power exploit national resources and steal; rule by a thief or thieves.*

2) *A society whose leaders make themselves rich and powerful by stealing from the rest of us.*

Today, kleptocracy is rampant not only in America but all over the world. Corruption is rampant in government, sports, education, business, and even religions. Today, there are many people who believe that Washington, D.C. stands for *District of Corruption*.

Financialization cannot take place without kleptocracy.

5. **The Baby Boom bust:** Baby boomers (1946 to 1964) caused much of the boom from 1971 to 2000. Unfortunately, baby boomers are no longer babies. They are now "senior citizens." Their peak spending years are over. Their McMansions will go on sale.

There is a saying, "Demography is Destiny." Much of *Rich Dad's Prophecy* was based on baby-boomer demographics. This generation's peak earning and spending years are behind them. They will live longer, act younger, and shake and rattle the global economy until 2050, many taking more out of the economy than they put in. There are 75 million American baby boomers.

The next baby boom is the millennial generation (1981-1997). There will be 81.1 million in the United States by 2036.

The Old and the New

The Western World is old; the New World is young. The New World is the emerging markets such as India, Vietnam, Middle East, South America, Africa, and Eastern Europe.

The New World is the millennial generation's world. They are tech savvy and born into a cyber world.

Just as American baby boomers shook up the world, the New-World millennial generation is already shaking up the world. Terrorism, vast migrations of people, Uber, AirBnB, and cyber warfare are the start of the changes.

The End of Growth

If you listen to financial experts, they always talk about "growth." The word *growth* makes hearts pound harder. The word *growth* makes people excited—"grow the economy"… "grow our wealth." After the crash of 2008, experts kept talking about "green shoots." That means they are looking for fresh growth.

Take another, closer look at 2008 on the chart of the Dow below, the low point.

120 Years of the Dow

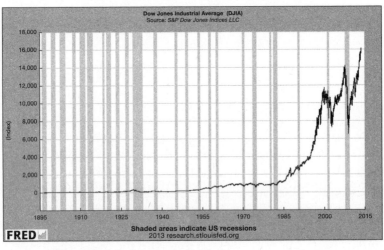

Source: FRED–Federal Reserve Economic Data

Savers really did become losers in 2008. That was the year the U.S Federal Reserve Bank began the biggest money printing operation in the history of world. And the printing has not stopped.

Warning to Savers… from Buffett

In September 2010, Warren Buffett had this to say to savers:

> *"The one thing I will tell you is the worst investment you can have is cash. Everybody is talking about cash being king and all that sort of thing. Cash is going to become worth less over time."*

Our leaders are still hoping for more green shoots, more growth. They hope printing more money will save the economy.

Lord Rothschild of the powerful Rothschild banking dynasty is often quoted as saying:

> *"This is the greatest experiment in monetary history in the history of the world."*

The Rothschild family should know. They set up the modern global banking system back in the 1760s in Germany.

Q: *Can our politicians save us?*

A: No. The problem is not political. It was Rothschild Bank founder Mayer Amschel Rothschild (1744-1812) who is credited with saying:

"Give me control of a nation's money and I care not who makes the laws."

Q: *So it makes very little difference if Republicans or Democrats are in control in Washington? The rich control the world?*

A: Correct. Always remember the golden rule:

"He who has the gold makes the rules."

Rich dad taught me to play by the rules of the rich. If you want to learn more about the rules of money the rich play by, read on.

Chapter Three

WHY TAXES MAKE THE RICH RICHER... LEGALLY

Poor Dad:

"Paying taxes is patriotic."

Rich Dad:

"Not paying taxes is patriotic."

During the 2012 Presidential election, President Obama told the world that he paid 30% in income taxes.

His opponent, Governor Mitt Romney, declared he paid 13% in income taxes.

Taxes were another nail in Mitt Romney's coffin in his bid for the U.S Presidency. Millions were outraged. Millions called him a crook and a cheat. Millions voted for Obama because they felt a bond with the Democratic candidate, believing "Obama is like me."

The word "ignorance" does not mean stupid. The base word of ignorance is "ignore." To ignore something means a person must actively *not want to know* something.

Definitions according to Merriam-Webster's Dictionary:

Ignorance: *Destitute of knowledge*

Ignore: *Refuse to take notice of*

Most of us know taxes are our greatest expense. Yet most people choose to *ignore the subject of tax.* They *choose to be ignorant,* then get angry at people like Romney who know how to make money and pay less in taxes—legally.

Without financial education, most people are financially ignorant about taxes. Many of these people vote for politicians who promise to "tax the rich." Then they wonder why their taxes keep going up. The problem is not taxes; the problem is spending.

One of the reasons for wealth and income inequality is tax. Simply stated, the rich do know how to make more money and pay less in taxes than the poor and middle class—legally. The rich are not always smarter, they simply prefer not to be ignorant.

Taxes Upon Taxes

There are more taxes than just income tax. There are taxes on taxes. It is estimated that for every dollar a person spends, 80% goes directly or indirectly to some kind of tax... and back to the government.

For example, if you pay a dollar for gasoline, not only is your dollar *net after tax,* which means your dollar has already been taxed, most of the money you pay for the gasoline is going to other levels of tax. The oil company receives very little of the dollar you used to purchase your gasoline. Then the oil company pays taxes on the tiny bit of *your dollar* they receive. Talk about *pennies on the dollar!*

I think many people would agree that the lack of financial education shows up in our political leaders. Most are employees, like my poor dad, people who know how to spend money but have no idea on how to make money. Financially ignorant leaders are at the core of this global crisis.

A Brief History Lesson

1773: The Boston Tea Party

It was a tax revolt—the spark that led to the Revolutionary War. In 1773, it was patriotic *not to pay taxes.*

Save for a few sets of circumstances and wars, like the Civil War, America was pretty much a no-tax or low-tax country from 1773 to 1943. Not paying taxes was patriotic. And America boomed.

1943: The Current Tax Payment Act

World War II was expensive. The government needed money to fight the war. The Current Tax Payment Act was passed as a "temporary tax."

The significance of this Act was that it was the first time the government was allowed to remove taxes directly from paychecks, before workers got paid. Talk about putting their hands in our pockets! This is one more reason the rich do not work for money.

After 1943, the government kept taking more and more from employees' paychecks. In the early 1960s, I remember opening my first paycheck and wondering where my money went.

The problem is that the 1943 Current Tax Payment Act was not temporary. It is now permanent. The government now has a legal vacuum cleaner sucking money out of your wallet.

Taxes Shorten Wars

If we really want world peace, just use taxes to pay for war.

In 1961, during his farewell address to the nation, President Dwight D. Eisenhower, former head of the Allied Forces in Europe, warned the world of the growing power of the military industrial complex.

America has been at war ever since.

Q: *Why has America been at war?*

A: War is profitable. War creates jobs and makes many people rich.

The Last War

Eisenhower, a 5-Star Army General, knew firsthand the horrors of war. He was the last President to fight a war with taxpayer dollars.

Q: *What is the importance of using taxpayer dollars to fight wars?*

A: Taxpayers demanded that the war end soon. Eisenhower knew taxpayers did not mind war, but they hated higher taxes. So taxes played a role in ending the Korean War.

Q: *How do we pay for wars today?*

A: America pays for wars with debt, not taxes. Future generations will eventually pay the taxes for today's wars.

Q: *Is that why Nixon took the dollar off the gold standard in 1971? The United States was spending too much money fighting in Vietnam?*

A: That was one of the reasons. The military industrial complex was spending money on a war we could not win. I know. I was there. War may be stupid, but war is profitable.

The poor and middle class send their sons and daughters to fight wars, and the rich get richer. I am afraid we are in a war on terror, a war that may never end. The rich on both sides are getting rich while innocent people die.

Q: *So taxes can be both patriotic and unpatriotic?*

A: Yes. It all depends upon your point of view… and your financial education.

Petrodollars

In 1974, President Nixon signed an agreement with the royal family of Saudi Arabia. The deal was that, from that point forward, all oil in the world must be traded in U.S. dollars. The U.S. dollar became the *Petrodollar.*

Q: *Why did they do that?*

A: Because after 1971, the year Nixon broke the promise to the world that the U.S. dollar would be backed by gold, the hegemony of the United States—the power and influence of the U.S. dollar—was threatened. By forcing the entire world to buy and sell oil in dollars, the United States and the dollar regained its status in the world.

Remember, oil is the lifeblood of the world economy. Oil replaced gold as money. The nations that controlled oil controlled the world. World War II was about oil. Japan attacked the United States because it cut Japan off from oil. Vietnam was about oil. The United States did not want Vietnam selling oil directly to China.

In 1999, the Euro was launched, threatening the power of the dollar. In 2000, Saddam Hussein declared he would start selling Iraq's oil to Europe in Euro, not dollars. In response to 9/11, the United States attacked Iraq, although most of the terrorists identified in the 9/11 attacks were from Saudi Arabia.

Did the same thing happen to Muammar Gaddafi, leader of Libya, the African nation with the largest oil reserves? In 2011, Gaddafi proposed the African and Muslim nations join together to create a new currency backed by gold, the dinar. The dinar would be used to buy and sell oil, in exclusion of the U.S. dollar. If his plan had worked, it would have disrupted the power of the central banking system of the world. In 2011, Gaddafi was dead.

Today ISIS and other terror networks are disrupting the world.

Q: *Why is the history of oil important?*

A: Taxes. Some of my biggest tax breaks come from investing in American oil.

Q: *You mean investing in oil companies like Chevron or Exxon?*

A: No. Those are investments for *passive* investors. I am a *professional* investor.

Q: *So passive investors do not receive the same tax breaks as professional investors receive?*

A: Correct. The tax rules are different. You will find out more as you read on. To be a professional investor, I suggest you seek professional tax advice.

Q: *Is investing in oil and receiving large tax large patriotic or unpatriotic?*

A: It doesn't matter what I think. What do you think?

Tax Lessons from Tom

Tax Breaks for Oil Development

Every country decides what is important to their economy. In the 1960s, the United States decided that oil independence was important to the U.S. economy. To encourage oil exploration and drilling, the U.S. Congress enacted two tax breaks for those who invested in U.S. oil exploration and drilling. The first tax break allows investors to deduct 100% of their investment into drilling new wells, about 80% of which is deducted in the first year or two of development. These are called intangible drilling costs. The second tax break allows investors to report only 85% of their income from drilling. This tax break is called percentage depletion. These two tax breaks combine to create an incentive for U.S. taxpayers to invest in U.S. oil and gas development projects, effectively becoming partners with the U.S. government on all exploration and drilling activities.

All Accountants Are Not Equal

Tom Wheelwright's contributions to this book are both important and valuable. Tom is the smartest CPA and tax strategist I have ever met, and I have met many.

Some CPAs are really stupid. Years ago, when I was just starting out, I asked a highly-respected CPA, *"How do I pay less in taxes?"* His reply *"Make less money."*

Another CPA, from a well-respected accounting firm advised me, *"You have too much real estate. I suggest you sell your real estate and put your money in stocks, bonds, and mutual funds."*

He said that in 2006. If I had followed his advice, I would have been wiped out in 2008.

Webster's Definitions

Merriam-Webster's Dictionary defines stupid as:

1) *slow of mind*

2) *given to unintelligent decisions*

Synonyms for stupid include: *dull, dense, and dumb.*

I know I am stupid in some respects. I know I have made stupid decisions—we all have. When it comes to taxes, I am very stupid. That is why I've paid these tax experts for their professional advice.

If not for my rich dad and my ongoing financial education, I might have followed stupid advice from CPAs.

This is another reason the rich are getting richer. The rich have smarter advisors than the poor and middle class.

Q: *So how does a person know a smart advisor from a stupid one?*

A: You have to get smarter first. If you do not know good advice from bad advice, any advice will do.

In all fairness, an advisor like a CPA can only give me advice to my level of education and experience. For example, if I cannot drive a car, I do not need racing lessons. I need to learn to drive a car first.

Better Tax Advice

Tom Wheelwright has been my personal advisor for years. Tom has guided me through the racetrack of life and business. He has made me and Kim millions and saved us millions in taxes. He has been one of our greatest teachers.

My point in saying this is that I had to get ready for Tom. He could not have guided me if I had not done my part first.

I asked Tom to write his book, *Tax-Free Wealth*, so you will know what you have to do, how you can prepare for the world of the rich.

> Q: *Are you saying, even if I have a college education and a good job, Tom cannot help me?*
>
> A: That is correct. In fact, if you are an employee, there is very little Tom can do for you. All you need is a tax preparation service like H&R Block.

Tax Lessons from Tom

Great Advisors Have Great Financial Education

When we get better financial education, our risk goes down as our results increase. This is true for advisors as well. When your tax advisor knows very little, your risk of an audit or of paying too much tax is very high. When your tax advisor knows a lot about the tax law, your risk of audit goes down as do your taxes.

Many people ask me if I am conservative or aggressive. I believe I am the most conservative tax advisor alive because I spend so much time every day studying the tax law. I like to show it like this:

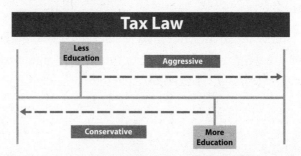

Who Pays the Highest Taxes?

Pictured below is the CASHFLOW Quadrant. That book, *Rich Dad's CASHFLOW Quadrant*, was the second book in the Rich Dad Series.

E stands for *employee.*

S stands for *self-employed, small business, or specialist* such as doctor, lawyer, real estate agent, or sports superstar.

B stands for a *big business* owner with 500 employees or more.

I stands for *investor: active investor not passive investor.*

The quadrant also tells the story of who pays the most—and least—in taxes.

TAX PERCENTAGES PAID PER QUADRANT

Q: *So after the Current Tax Payment Act of 1943, anyone who works for money pays the highest taxes?*

A: Yes. That is why rich dad's money rule #1 is: The Rich Don't Work for Money.

Q: *So professional investors pay the least in taxes?*

A: Yes.

Q: *I am an investor. I have a retirement plan. I invest through my company pension. And I have a small portfolio of stocks, bonds, mutual funds, and ETFs. I have tax-free returns. And I am ex-military and I have a military pension. Am I in the I quadrant?*

A: No. You are probably a *passive investor. Professional investors* are different. Think of it this way: One of the great golfers in history is Tiger Woods. Even if I used Tiger Woods' golf clubs and wore Tiger Woods' shirt and shoes, I would still never be a *professional golfer* like Tiger Woods.

In other words, professional investing is not about the investment. It is the about the investor. And the financial education required to live life in the I quadrant is massive.

Q: *Do you think I can do it?*

A: That is up to you. Only you can answer that question.

Tax Lessons from Tom

Consumers vs. Producers

Think of the E, S, B, and I quadrants in terms of consuming and producing. Someone in the E quadrant produces whatever they can produce by themselves and consumes an equal amount. Someone in the S quadrant produces a little more (if they have some employees) and consumes a little less than they produce. Someone in the B or I quadrant, however, produces much more than they consume. In the B quadrant, they are creating hundreds or thousands of jobs, and in the I quadrant they are producing energy, food, and housing. They still only consume the same amount as someone in the E or S quadrant. The government encourages and rewards these activities through tax breaks because the producers stimulate the economy and produce the food, fuel, and housing that the rest of the citizens need to live happy, productive lives.

The B and I Quadrants

There are rich people in all four quadrants. There are many rich employees and self-employed specialists such as doctors, lawyers, sports stars and artists. In the E and S quadrants there are both rich and poor people.

The richest people in the world live in the I quadrant. There are no poor people in the I quadrant. The amount of wealth they have may vary, but no one is poor.

Q: *So why do they pay the least in taxes, if they are rich?*

A: Because of the golden rule: *"He who has the gold makes the rules."*

Q: *So you play by the rules of the I quadrant?*

A: I do. And so can you. The rules do not discriminate.

Q: *And the rules for the E quadrant are different?*

A: Very different.

> Q: *How long did it take you to get to the I quadrant?*
>
> A: It took a while. Nothing happens overnight.

In 1973, I returned from Vietnam. My poor dad suggested I go back to school and get my Master's degree and live my life in the E quadrant. My rich dad suggested I take a real estate investment course so I could one day live my life in the I quadrant.

> Q: *What did you do?*
>
> A: I did both. I flew for the Marines during the day and started night school for my MBA. I also took a 3-day course on real estate investing.

> Q: *What happened?*
>
> A: I dropped out of the MBA program after six months.

> Q: *Why?*
>
> A: There were many reasons. One reason was the instructors. The instructors in the MBA program had no real world experience. They were professional teachers teaching business courses.

The real estate course instructor was a real, real estate investor. He inspired me to learn. The MBA instructors were boring. The real estate instructor was teaching me about the I quadrant. The MBA instructors were teaching me about the E quadrant. After six months, I was gone—because I knew where I wanted to go. I wanted to one day live my life in the I quadrant as a professional investor.

The 3-day real estate course, 40-plus years ago, cost $385, which for me, at the time, was half my monthly income as a Marine pilot. The course did not give me answers. The course taught me what I needed to learn, and what I needed to do after the class was over. Today, I am still a student and still learning.

> Q: *What was your return on the $385?*
>
> A: Millions. Most importantly I learned to use debt and taxes to become rich.

Q: *Debt and taxes have made you rich?*

A: Yes. And it's the same *debt* and *taxes* that make most people poor. *Debt* and *taxes* make those with financial education richer. The knowledge gained from that $385 course was priceless.

Q: *Should I go back to school?*

A: The type of school you attend depends upon which quadrant you want to live your life in. I wanted to live my life in the I quadrant, the same quadrant where the richest people in the world live. Once I completed that 3-day real estate course, I kept on learning and continued to take classes. I love learning in the I quadrant.

Q: *Do you think people should enter the MBA program?*

A: Absolutely—especially today. MBA programs provide a solid foundation for all quadrants. Once you graduate, then they can decide which quadrant they want to live in. Keep in mind that it's not the profession that determines the quadrant. For example, a medical doctor could be an employee in the E quadrant, a doctor in private practice in the S quadrant, build a hospital in the B quadrant, and become a professional investor in the I quadrant.

The difference is the mindset, skillsets, and financial education. If you want to live your life in the B and I quadrants, you must know how to use *debt* and *taxes* to get richer.

Q: *So your 3-day real estate course was your entry into the I quadrant?*

A: Yes. But I can't stress this enough: that 3-day course was just the start. My instructor inspired me to learn more and I kept on learning. I took courses on stock trading, foreign exchange trading, options trading, gold and silver investing, financial planning, debt, taxes, and how to raise capital as well as different levels of real estate courses, from buying

small homes to developing property. I love learning in the
I quadrant.

If you have ever seen the TV program *Shark Tank,* you've seen what
real people in the I quadrant do. They look at investments, business
or real estate, and start-ups, and then decide if the product and the
entrepreneurs are worth funding.

Q: *Is that what I-quadrant people do?*

A: Yes, it is a great life. It sure beats working.

Q: *How long did it take you to get to the I quadrant?*

A: I was 47 and Kim was 37 when we were financially free.
There were many bumps along the way. Kim and I were
homeless for a short while. In the process we achieved
not only wealth and freedom, but we gained education,
knowledge, wisdom, experience, and friends who think like
we do.

Q: *How long will it take me?*

A: That depends upon you. I have met a number of people
who are naturals in the I quadrant. I wasn't, so it took me a
while. Kim is a natural. She loves her life in the I quadrant.

Taxes Are Incentives

The point I want to make is that people on the E and S side of the
CASHFLOW Quadrant pay the highest percentages in taxes. There is
little a person like Tom can do for them, unless they are first willing to
invest in their financial education.

I have met so many successful accountants, attorneys, and doctors
who will tell me and Tom, "You can't do that here." No matter where
we are in the world, some expert will raise his or her hand and say,
"You can't do that here. It's illegal."

The problem is that these experts are locked into the mindset of
their quadrant. It requires financial education to move from the left
side, the E and S side, to the B and I side.

In 1994, after Kim and I made it to the I quadrant, she and I formed The Rich Dad Company in the B quadrant. The purpose for starting The Rich Dad Company was to provide financial education for those who wanted to migrate from the E and S quadrants and become Bs and Is. As you know, there are no guarantees that anyone will make it to the B and I quadrants.

Our first product was the CASHFLOW® game, which was released in 1996, followed by *Rich Dad Poor Dad* in 1997. In 2000, *Rich Dad Poor Dad* made *The New York Times* list and remained on the list for more than six years. A month later, Oprah called and I was her guest for her entire hour-long show. That day changed my life and the course of The Rich Dad Company.

I have been called an "overnight success" many times. In some ways that is true. In just one hour—talking to Oprah and her millions of loyal fans, telling the story of my two dads, one rich and one poor, and the importance of financial education—I went from unknown to world famous. Yet I assure you, there was a lot of hard work and study… long before Oprah called.

A Final Word on Taxes

The reason Governor Mitt Romney paid 13% in taxes and President Obama paid 30% is because Romney operates out of the B and I quadrants. Barack Obama operates out of the E and S quadrants. They see the world very differently.

That is the power of real financial education.

Incentives

When Tom and I teach together, on stages all over the world, he explains that taxes and tax breaks are incentives. And incentives are different for the different quadrants.

For example, people in the E and S quadrants respond to the incentive of more money, more income, higher pay, and bonuses. Those in the E and S quadrants work for money.

People on the B and I side work for tax incentives. They make more money, indirectly, via tax breaks.

For example, B-quadrant people receive tax breaks for hiring employees. The government does this because the government needs jobs for people. There's a steady stream of tax dollars flowing into government coffers from employee paychecks. So the government offers the incentive of lower taxes. These are entrepreneurs such as Elon Musk. He receives billions in tax breaks from different states and from the U.S. government.

In the I quadrant, I receive tax breaks for investing in apartment complexes. If I did not provide housing, the government would have to, costing taxpayers a lot of money. So rather than ask taxpayers to pay higher taxes, the government offers entrepreneurs like me tax incentives. I become a partner with the government.

If the government had to build those apartment buildings... that would be Socialism. If I build them, it's Capitalism. Personally, I prefer to be a Capitalist on the B and I side of the CASHFLOW Quadrant.

Tax Lessons from Tom

Government Incentives

Even the E and S quadrants receive tax incentives. In the United States, for example, those who purchase houses can deduct the interest expense on their tax return. Those who save for retirement can deduct their investments through IRAs, RRSPs, and Superannuations. Those who give to charity can deduct their donations. These are all tax incentives from the government.

The B and the I quadrants simply receive many more tax incentives from the government because the activities that take place in those quadrants perform vital functions that help the government do its job of improving the economy, providing jobs, and providing food, energy, and fuel to citizens and businesses.

Now you may understand why Tom Wheelwright is my tax advisor and my adjuvant on this book. He makes sure I do the right things in business and that what I write about is accurate. I have no desire to go to jail or to misinform you.

The reason Tom is my personal advisor is because every investment or business is different. Most deals do not work and we turn them down. But with every business opportunity or property deal we do our due diligence on, we become smarter together.

Remember this: People who say, *"You can't do that here,"* probably live their lives in the E or S quadrants. So it is true, most of them *cannot* do it there. But you *can*, if you invest in your financial education for the B and I quadrants.

Tax Lessons from Tom

You Can't Do That Here

When I hear this, I am hearing that the person speaking is saying that you can't do this in their situation. They are correct. In order to do what Robert and I do, you have to change your situation. For example, someone who rents their house cannot deduct their house payments (rent) whereas someone who owns their house can (interest). So in order to deduct a house payment, a person has to change their situation from a renter to a homeowner. The same is true with other deductions, credits and tax benefits. A person must place themselves in the right situation in order to obtain the tax benefit. If they do, it doesn't matter if they are wealthy or not, they will get the tax benefit. The wealthy simply have learned to place themselves in the right situation more often than the poor and middle class.

Later in this book, Tom and I will guide you through real deals that Kim and I have done—deals that Es and Ss cannot do.

Chapter Four

WHY MISTAKES MAKE THE RICH RICHER

Poor Dad:
"Mistakes make you stupid."

Rich Dad:
"Mistakes make you smarter."

Have you ever watched a baby learning to walk? The baby stands, wobbles, then takes a step. Oftentimes the baby falls. And cries. We all know the next steps. Soon the baby is at it again, getting up from the floor, standing, wobbling, falling again and, quite likely, crying again, too. The baby repeats the process until one day he or she walks, then runs, rides a bicycle, drives a car, and leaves home.

This is the way god designed us to learn. Humans learn by making mistakes. If the baby were punished each time he or she fell, the baby would crawl for the rest of its life. The baby would never leave home.

In school, students learn by lecture, reading, and studying and then take a test. Let's say there are 10 questions on the test and the student makes three mistakes. The teacher awards a grade of 70%, and the class moves on to the next lesson.

The school system discards the most important part of the test, *the mistakes*. Rather than learn from their mistakes, students are punished for making them. Many students leave school feeling stupid (certainly not smart!) and fearful of mistakes, less self-confident about their ability to learn.

Mistakes tell the teacher what a student does not know and, in many cases, what the teacher failed to teach. Mistakes are opportunities for both student and teacher to get smarter.

A year after graduation, most students have forgotten 75% of the "right" answers. What they never forget are the negative messages: "Don't make mistakes. People who make mistakes are stupid."

Rich dad had a tremendous respect for mistakes. He often said, "Mistakes are god's way of talking to you. Mistakes are saying, 'Wake up. Pay attention. There is something you need to know.'"

After school, rich dad's son and I worked in his business two days a week. After work, he would sit down with us to debrief and discuss the day. He wanted to know what we learned, what we did not understand, and what mistakes we made. If we did make mistakes, he wanted us to tell the truth. He did not want us to learn to lie about them. And he believed mistakes are only sins when not admitted.

Tax Lessons from Tom

Specialists Hate Making Mistakes

Accountants, attorneys, doctors, Internet gurus, and other professionals usually stay in the E or the S quadrants. They work so hard to be right, it's very difficult for them to be wrong and admit their mistakes. This is why so few of them make it to the B or the I quadrants. They just don't understand the benefits of making mistakes and allowing others to make mistakes. This is what holds them back.

The Best Teachers in the World

Rich dad's homework assignments were reading books about entrepreneurs. After finishing a book, we would get together for a "book study" and discuss what we learned. We read some great books about great entrepreneurs. Rich dad often said, "The best teachers in the world are in books."

One of my favorite books of those we studied was about the life of Thomas Edison. Edison, who lived from 1847 to 1931, was an inventor and founder of corporate giant, General Electric.

In school, Edison's teachers said he was "too stupid to learn" and that he was "addled." He left school and was educated by his mom at home where he had the time to study what he wanted to study.

One of his creations was the prototype for today's modern laboratory. In his laboratory, people could *experiment as a team—and he and his team had the freedom to fail together until they succeeded.*

Some of the inventions to come out of his laboratory were the telegraph, phonograph, electric light bulb, alkaline storage battery, and a camera for motion pictures—inventions that changed the world. Not bad for a student who was too stupid to learn.

My favorite Edison quote is:

"I have not failed. I've just found 10,000 ways that won't work."

And to people who quit he said:

"Many of life's failures are people who did not realize how close they were to success when they gave up."

Many of you have heard these two quotes by Edison before. Yet I ask you, how much of your life is limited by your fear of making mistakes, your fear of failing? What about fear of being fired, fear of not having a job, and fear of looking stupid?

The Millionaire Next Door

Between 1971 and 2000 people did not need to change. They were protected by a rising global economy.

In 1996, *The Millionaire Next Door* was published. It was a runaway bestseller, a reflection of the euphoria the world was experiencing.

The middle class loved this book. It defined the *millionaire* as a middle-class, college graduate with a good job and a house in the suburbs. These *millionaires* drove modest cars like Volvos and Toyotas and followed the financial planners' formula that prescribed "*Save money, get out of debt, and invest for the long term in a well-diversified portfolio of stocks, bonds, and mutual funds.*"

The millionaire next door became a millionaire by being in the right place, doing the right things, at the right time in history. The problem is that these *millionaires next door did not need financial education to become a millionaire.*

Then the World Changed…

If we look again at the 120-year chart of the Dow on page 34, we can see the bottom fell out soon after *The Millionaire Next Door* was published in 1996. By 2008, many of the millionaires next door were *The Foreclosures Next Door.*

Rich Dad Poor Dad was published in 1997, with the opposite message. *Rich Dad Poor Dad* was about what the rich knew that *the millionaire next door* did not.

In 2008, the world nearly collapsed and the governments of the world began printing trillions of dollars to keep the economy afloat. Many *millionaires next door* were spared from financial ruin. They were millionaires on paper… "net worth millionaires." They were "home equity millionaires." And "retirement account millionaires." The problem was, most had little to no financial education. In many ways, the same is true today.

Today, rather than looking ahead and planning for retirement, many of these *millionaires next door* are worried about losing everything, They know something is very wrong in the economy. Many worry about living longer and running out of money in retirement.

What If I Fail?

This chapter is about mistakes. What most people learn in school is the fear of making mistakes. Their fear becomes a mental wall, a divider between what they know and what they need to learn.

At the beginning of this book, I wrote about people asking me, "What should I do with my money?" Many people who asked that question are in trouble today.

Q: *Why are they in trouble?*

A: Because they are people who saved money, bought a house, got out of debt, and invested for the long term in the stock market.

Q: *Those are the people who may be wiped out?*

A: Yes.

Q: *What can they do?*

A: They do have options. But when I suggest they get a real financial education, rather than turning their money over to experts, most say:

But what if I fail?

What if I make a mistake?

What if I lose money?

Isn't that risky?

Won't that be a lot of work?

I don't have to worry. I have Social Security.

Q: *So you cannot teach them anything if they are afraid of failing? Or they don't want to learn?*

A: That's correct. The days of *the millionaire next door* are over. Gone are the days when you could turn your money over to an *expert* and wake up a millionaire.

Another of Lord Rothschild's statements comes across as a dire warning: *"The six months under review have seen central bankers continuing what is surely the greatest experiment in monetary policy in the history of the world. We are therefore in uncharted waters and it is impossible to predict the unintended consequences of very low interest rates, with some 30% of the global government debt at negative yields, combined with quantitative easing on a massive scale."*

Q: *What does that mean?*

A: It means the world is in serious trouble.

Between 1971 and 2000 people who had good jobs, saved money, and were passive investors in the stock market were the big winners.

Just before retiring, the millionaires next door shifted to bonds for steady income during retirement. Between 1971 and 2000, bonds were bulletproof—virtually guaranteed safe and secure.

Today savers are losers, the stock market is in the biggest bubble in world history, and bonds, once safe and secure, are time bombs. If interest rates start going back up, the bond market may blow up.

Weapons of Mass Destruction

Earlier in this book, I stated that one reason for the growing gap between the rich and everyone else is *financialization,* the production of toxic money and synthetic assets, sometimes called *derivatives.* Or, as Warren Buffett calls them: *"financial weapons of mass destruction."*

And Buffett should know. His company, Moody's, blessed these "weapons of mass destruction"—MBS, mortgage backed securities. A MBS is made up of *subprime* mortgages from poor people. Then financial engineers take over, and like magic, turn *subprime* into *prime.*

After Moody's blessed these weapons of mass destruction as "safe and sound," they were sold into the world economy. The explosion that followed rocked the financial world.

Q: *Derivatives could not have been sold without Moody's blessing?*

A: Correct. Buffett and friends made billions while millions of people's lives were destroyed in the blast. Then friends in government bailed out Buffett and friends with trillions in taxpayer money. This is kleptocracy in its finest hour.

Q: *So it was financially engineered derivatives, synthetic assets that caused the real estate market to crash in 2007 and the banking crash of 2008?*

A: Yes. The real estate market did not crash---derivatives began exploding and the world nearly came crashing down.

If you want to learn more about derivatives and their destructive power, the movie, *The Big Short* does a great job keeping you entertained while educating you about financial weapons of mass destruction.

You can watch me on CNN, in a 2008 interview with
Wolf Blitzer, warning of the looming crash and the fall
of Lehman Brothers, one of the oldest banks in America.
I issued the warning six months before the crash.
You can see this video by going to:
RichDad.com/RDTV

But Wait... It Gets Worse

In 2007, before the crash, there were $700 trillion in derivatives about to explode. Today, there are $1.2 quadrillion.

Q: *What if they go off again?*

A: This time the millionaire next door may be wiped out.

Q: *Are they safe today?*

A: No. On September 1, 2016, *The Wall Street Journal* wrote about the troubles of the mighty Deutsche Bank. Once the most powerful bank in the world, founded in 1870 and staffed by over 100,000 employees worldwide, the banking giant is selling parts of its business to raise money. Negative interest rates are like a cancer on a bank's business model. *The Wall Street Journal* also noted that the bank's derivate portfolio is starting to overheat, approaching meltdown, like the Fukushima nuclear reactors did in Japan in 2011.

Q: *Is there an easier way to understand derivatives?*

A: Think of an orange. Orange juice is a derivative of the orange. Orange juice concentrate is a derivative of orange juice.

A *mortgage loan* is a *financial derivative of a house.*

What the financial engineers did was take millions of mortgages and turn them into *mortgage concentrate* and sell this toxic concentrate to the world. As long as subprime borrowers, in some cases people without jobs, could make their monthly mortgage payments, the world was safe and secure.

Atomic War

An atomic bomb is a derivative of the chemical element uranium, symbol U, atomic number 92. As a kid in school during the 1960s, everyone lived in fear of atomic war. We were told Russia and China were our enemies and that they were going to attack us.

In response to this atomic threat, we had ridiculous atomic-bomb drills in school. On our teachers' command, little kids crawled under their desks and covered their heads.

Today, foreign powers continue their sabre rattling. Atomic bombs and other weapons of mass destruction are real threats. Decimating ISIS and global terrorism threats are imperatives. Kleptocracy runs rampant in the world's governments, global corporations, central banks, and the financial services industry. And today there is still little if any financial education in our schools.

Prisoners of the E Quadrant

In many cases, school sets us up for life. It's both a foundation and a mindset that—without new ideas that rock people's boats—the die is cast.

When a parent says to a child, "Go to school and get a job," the child is being programmed for life in the E quadrant.

The problem is that, for most people, the E quadrant is the *only* quadrant they ever think about. Most people have no idea there is a bigger world outside the E quadrant.

We are all *humans*, but very different *beings*. The *beings* in the E quadrant all say the same words, in different languages, all over the world. They all say, "I want a safe secure job, a steady paycheck, good benefits, and time off." It does not matter if the *being* speaks English, Spanish, Japanese, German, or Swahili… the words are the same.

A Being... Being Human

A human being is made up of four basic components. They are:

1. Mind
2. Body
3. Emotions
4. Spirit

Our current educational system is designed to program a student's mind, body, emotions, and spirit into a *being* who is an employee.

Q: *Is that why it's so hard for employees to give up job security and a steady paycheck? Without real financial education, the emotion of fear runs them?*

A: Absolutely. Without financial education, a *being* can only be human.

Q: *Is that why there is no financial education in our schools?*

A: That's my opinion, based upon what my research tells me. The Western system of education is based on the Prussian system, an educational system designed to produce workers and soldiers, people trained to follow orders and do what they are told to do.

I am not saying it's bad to follow orders. I follow orders. I obey the law. A person must be a good follower before he or she can become a good leader. When people stop obeying rules and laws we have chaos.

My concern is that our educational system uses fear to teach. That is why people cannot think. They worry more about making mistakes, failing, and looking foolish. Without high EQ, emotional intelligence, and financial education, most people leave school and become prisoners in the E quadrant. They cannot escape.

The Torture Chamber

After graduating from college, many A students go on to graduate and professional schools, becoming *specialists* in the S quadrant. They become doctors, accountants, and lawyers.

Many others become *self-employed* professionals in the S quadrant. They become real estate salespeople, massage therapists, computer programmers, web designers, actors, artists, and musicians. Some do exceptionally well financially, but most do not.

Others become *small business owners* in the S quadrant. They may start a restaurant, open a boutique, or a fitness studio.

Q: *Why do you call the S Quadrant "the Torture Chamber?"*

A: Because it is the worst quadrant. The first thing that happens to a person who leaves the E quadrant is that expenses go up and income goes down. Then government rules and regulations are piled on you. You have no benefits—no medical and dental insurance, retirement plans, or paid vacations. Your income goes down because you are no longer doing your job, which is to take care of your customers. Your *new* job is running and building a business and dealing with people who take your time and your money.

Q: *Is that why nine out of 10 businesses fail in the first five years?*

A: Yes.

Q: *Does it get better after the business is built?*

A: A little, but the torture never ends for the S-quadrant entrepreneur.

For example, those in the S quadrant will always pay the highest taxes, 60% or higher in some states. In many cases, that is why most stay small. The extra income is not worth the hassle of making more money.

Q: *What is the good news?*

A: The good news is there are many more programs teaching people to be entrepreneurs. Today, many schools are offering entrepreneur programs, ways to make the transition from E to S less risky.

The bad news is, most programs are designed to teach people to be S-quadrant entrepreneurs.

Q: *What are the benefits of being successful in the S quadrant?*

A: The S quadrant is the most important quadrant.

Q: *Why?*

A: If you succeed, you become a real entrepreneur. And you'll never go back to the E quadrant.

The Best News

If you become rich and successful in the S-quadrant, you are qualified to move on to the B and I quadrants. That is what Ray Kroc did when he bought McDonald's from the McDonald brothers. He took the brothers' business from the S quadrant to the B and I quadrants… and made billions.

Q: *Have you done the same thing?*

A: Yes. Not on the scale of McDonald's, but the path I followed is similar. I am not yet a billionaire.

Q: *Was the process of going from being an employee in the E quadrant, then to the S quadrant, then to the B and I quadrants difficult?*

A: For me, the journey between quadrants was extremely difficult.

Q: *Why?*

A: Because the education for each *being* in each quadrant is different. The lessons are different and so are the personal challenges.

When I transitioned from E to S my *being* had to change. I had to scramble and learn what I did not know. I had no steady paycheck, but I had employees who needed paychecks and benefits. I had to buy desks and office equipment. I had to raise money from investors to buy inventory for my nylon and Velcro wallet business. Every mistake I made, or mistakes my employees made, cost me money.

Just as a baby falls before it walks, I fell everyday—and had to pick myself up. If not for my rich dad teaching me to respect the lesson in every mistake, I would have quit. I would have become what Edison called a "*failure.*" Repeating his quote:

> *"Many of life's failures are people who did not realize how close they were to success when they gave up."*

I had to go beyond failure before I succeeded. That is how our *being* transforms and changes quadrants.

Once I succeeded in the S quadrant I was ready to take on the B and I quadrants. Every successful entrepreneur I know has gone through the same process.

Q: *When will I learn about the B and I quadrants?*

A: That is what the rest of this book is about.

For now I want you to begin to understand the difference between *human failures* and *rich beings.*

What It Takes

Changing quadrants requires four things:

1. **Spiritual intelligence**… your quiet intelligence knows there is a greater person in you, a person who can achieve their dreams.

2. **Mental intelligence…** the knowledge that you can learn anything you want to learn.

3. ***Emotional intelligence...*** your ability to learn from your mistakes. In certain situations, emotional intelligence is at least three times more powerful than mental intelligence, especially when you are angry. Resist blaming others, even if it was their fault. Blame is a sign of low emotional intelligence. Blame stands for *Be Lame,* a lame being. Remember all coins have three sides, heads, tails, and the edge. Emotional intelligence is the ability to stand on the edge of the coin and learn from the two sides.

4. ***Physical intelligence...*** your ability to take what you learn, turn your ideas into action, and stand back up when you fall.

If you can engage all four of your intelligences, you will win—no matter what happens in the economy.

If you can do it everyday, no matter what happens, you will become a strong and great person, greater than you are today.

Chapter Five

WHY CRASHES MAKE THE RICH RICHER

Poor Dad:

"I hope the market does not crash."

Rich Dad:

"I do not care if the market crashes."

If **Walmart** was having a 50%-off Sale, you could not get into the store. If **Wall Street** has a 50%-off sale, *the millionaire next door* runs and hides.

The Planet's Friendly Genius

In 1983, I read the book *Grunch of Giants,* written by Dr. R. Buckminster Fuller. After reading that book, I could see the coming of the financial crisis we are in today.

Dr. Fuller is often called The Planet's Friendly Genius. He is best known for designing the geodesic dome.

In 1967, I hitchhiked from my school at Kings Point in New York to Montreal, Canada to Expo '67, the World's Fair themed Man and His World. I especially wanted to see Dr. Fuller's massive geodesic dome, the U.S. Pavilion at the Expo. The dome was unbelievable.

In 1981, I had the opportunity to study with Bucky Fuller for a week at a ski resort in Kirkwood, California. That week changed the direction of my life.

I studied with him again in 1982 and 1983. He was teaching our class how we could predict the future. Dr. Fuller passed away a few weeks after that last event.

Fuller was known for many things. He was a scientist, an architect, a mathematician and a futurist. Many of his predictions have come true with uncanny accuracy. For example, he predicted a new technology would come into this world before or around 1990. On schedule, the Internet arrived in 1989 as the ARPANET, six years after Fuller's passing.

His book *Grunch of Giants* was released in 1983. GRUNCH is an acronym standing for <u>Gr</u>oss <u>U</u>niversal <u>C</u>ash <u>H</u>eist. In that book, he explained how the ultra-rich are ripping off the world and what the future holds for all of us. Bucky was saying the same things my rich dad had been telling me for years.

Who Is GRUNCH?

Fuller writes in *Grunch*:

> *"Who runs GRUNCH? Nobody knows. It controls all the world's banks. Even the muted Swiss banks. It does what its lawyers tell it to do. It maintains technical legality, and is prepared to prove it. Its law firm is named Machiavelli, Machiavelli, Atoms & Oil. Some think the second Mach is a cover for Mafia."*

The most important point I want to make is that we should all be aware of the fact that the game of money is rigged. It is not fair. The game of money that GRUNCH plays is to steal our wealth, via our money, our monetary system.

The World Is Waking Up

Quoting *The Economist*, from March 26, 2016:

> *"America used to be the land of opportunity and optimism. Now opportunity is seen as the preserve of the elite: two-thirds of Americans believed the economy is rigged in favor of vested interests. And optimism has turned to anger."*

> *"America is meant to be a temple of free enterprise. It isn't."*

> *"The game may indeed be rigged."*

Q: *Can we stop GRUNCH?*

A: You could try. But rather than take on GRUNCH, I decided to learn and understand the game GRUNCH plays. I decided I wouldn't be a victim. That is why, in 1963 I began to look into the future… and chose not to play the game GRUNCH wants us to play.

Q: *What game is that?*

A: The game that begins with the instructions "Go to school, work hard, pay taxes, get out of debt, and save money."

To beat GRUNCH I knew I had to learn to see the future—and prepare for the future.

How to See the Future

The way to see the future is to study the past. Fuller called it *prognostication.*

Let me teach you how Dr. Fuller taught me to see the future. Let's use the same 120-year chart of the Dow that we've already studied:

120 Years of the Dow

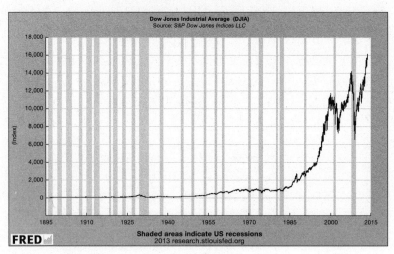

Source: FRED–Federal Reserve Economic Data

You will now learn how to see the future by simply looking, again, at the past 20 years of the Dow Jones Industrial Average.

1913:

Federal Reserve Bank is created.

In that same year:

The 16th Amendment to the U.S. Constitution was passed, authorizing the government to tax income.

> Q: *The Fed was created the same year income tax was created?*
>
> A: Yes. The Fed needs tax dollars to create dollars.

Tax Lessons from Tom

Tax Dollars Create New Dollars

The Fed can only create dollars because these dollars are backed by the U.S. taxpayer. Without the tax system, the Fed would have no backing and could not create dollars.

Q: *Why is this date so important?*

A: Because it was in 1913 that today's global crisis began. Today's financial crisis would not have happened without the creation of the Federal Reserve System and the IRS, the tax system.

Many experts agree that without the Fed, there would not have been multi-trillions in *quantitative easing*, the printing of money. Without the Fed, there would not have been the 2007 real estate market crash.

Without the Fed, the giant banks would not have crashed in 2008. And without the Fed, the giant banks could not have been bailed out with taxpayer money.

That is why 1913 is an important date in understanding the history behind today's crisis.

1929:

The giant stock market crash. This crash led to the Great Depression. The Depression terrified the American people. Their financial insecurity led to the Great Society, the genesis of many of the social programs we have today, including the unfunded liabilities of entitlement programs that are bankrupting America today.

The national debt of the United States, in 2017, is estimated to be over $220 trillion, when off-balance-sheet liabilities, the insolvent programs like Social Security and Medicare, are included.

1935:

Social Security is enacted by President Franklin D. Roosevelt. Today, millions are counting on the government to take care of them when they retire.

1943:

Current Tax Payment Act is passed, whereby Congress authorized taxes to be taken from employees' paychecks before the employee, in the E quadrant, is paid.

1944:

The Bretton Woods Agreement puts the world on the *dollar standard*. The United States agrees to back its dollar with gold. The world is required to trade internationally in U.S. dollars.

Instead of saving gold, the Central Banks of the world were required to save U.S. dollars. The dollar was now "as good as gold" and became the "reserve currency of the world." This gave the United States an unprecedented advantage in the world economy and America—and many Americans—became extremely rich.

1971:

President Richard Nixon violates the Bretton Woods Agreement. The printing of money begins. Today's crisis could not have happened if Nixon had not violated the Bretton Woods Agreement.

1972:

President Nixon opens the doors to China. Job security is lost to lower wage countries.

In three decades, China went from a dirt-poor country to a world power.

1974:

President Nixon signs Petrodollar Agreement with Saudi Arabia. The U.S. dollar is now backed by oil. All countries must now buy oil in U.S. dollars… which makes the U.S. dollar the most powerful currency in history.

Petrodollars allowed the Fed to print money like mad men. The good news is that the U.S. economy boomed. The bad news is that terrorism is increasing.

Thousands of people are dying at the hands of terrorists and millions more are fleeing their homelands, displaced by war… war caused, in large part, by the Petrodollar.

The U.S. government's position, oftentimes, is that it is the World's Policeman. That is not really true. America fights wars to protect the hegemony of the U.S. dollar.

Q: *What does hegemony mean?*

A: Hegemony is the authority of one nation over others. The agreement with Saudi Arabia and other oil producers gave Americans a stronger economy, an incredible lifestyle, a higher standard of living, and an unfair advantage over other people of the world.

Q: *What happens if the Petrodollar as currency comes to an end?*

A: Good question. No one really knows. Trillions of Petrodollars will *probably* come home, as Central Banks dump their dollar reserves… which *may* cause massive hyperinflation in America. America's hegemony will come to an end and the gap between rich and poor will grow wider.

Q: *So the crisis in the Middle East started in 1973, when the dollar became a Petrodollar? You mean millions of people are migrating to Europe because of the Petrodollar?*

A: A thoughtful question. You are now learning how to see the future by studying the past.

1978:

The 401(k) is created. Today, 80% of all baby boomers feel they will become poorer in retirement. The 401(k) was not designed to make the baby boomers financially secure. The 401(k) was designed to make Wall Street richer.

1983:

Bucky Fuller's *Grunch of Giants* is published.

1987:

The stock market crashes. Fed Chairman Alan Greenspan (1987-2006) enacts The Greenspan Put. Its official name is President's Working Group on Financial Markets. Insiders call it the Plunge Protection Team.

> Q: *What does the Plunge Protection Team do?*
> A: Every time markets crash, money from "mysterious sources," sources that many suspect are funded by the Fed, rushes in to prop up the market.

Once Greenspan and the Fed prevented the 1987 crash, the rich knew the Fed was standing behind them. They rich could not lose.

Look at 1987 and you will see that the markets took off after Greenspan signaled he would be *their banker*. The Fed issued a "money back" guarantee to the rich—a safety net of sorts, if the markets crashed. The rich could not lose.

1987 to 2000:

The Dow goes parabolic. And the millionaire next door gets rich.

Millions of middle class, passive investors become millionaires via inflation in the value of their homes, their 401(k)s, and IRAs as well as company and government pension plans. It was very easy for Americans to "get rich" between 1970 and 2000.

1996:

The book *The Millionaire Next Door* is published. Author Thomas Stanley praises the average person who becomes a millionaire by buying a house, living frugally, and investing for the long term in the stock market.

Fed Chairman Alan Greenspan warns of "irrational exuberance." His words were a signal that the party was coming to an end. He should know. He and the Fed financed the party. "Irrational exuberance" was his way of saying, "Boys, you're drunk. I'm going to take the 'punch bowl' away."

1997:

Rich Dad Poor Dad is published, warning that the rich don't work for money, savers are losers, and your house is not an asset.

> Q: *Did you write Rich Dad Poor Dad as a warning?*
>
> A: Yes. I was warning that the "sleigh ride" was over. The boom was about to bust. And the cash heist was about to begin.
>
> Q: *Are you saying the baby-boom generation may become the baby-bust generation?*
>
> A: Yes. Today, as I write in 2017, the middle class is shrinking and poverty is increasing.

Take a moment to study the graph on the following page. It shows the history—and the solvency status—of Social Security in the United States. What do you see in the future… for baby boomers, their children, and their grandchildren?

Social Security Surpluses and Deficits

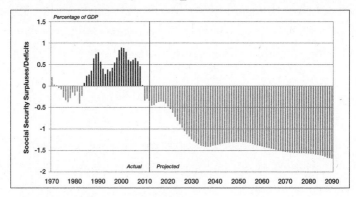

Source: Peter G. Peterson Foundation

You are now a prognosticator. What do you see as you look into the future?

1999:

The European Union creates the Euro.

2000:

Saddam Hussein announces his intention to sell Iraqi oil in Euros.

2001:

The World Trade Center is attacked. Fourteen of the 19 hijackers are from Saudi Arabia. None were from Iraq.

Flashback… to June 28, 1914:

Archduke Franz Ferdinand is assassinated in Sarajevo and World War I begins. On that same day, England signed an agreement for the oil rights in Mesopotamia, known today as Iraq. Mosul was an important city in 1914 and it is an important city today. Today, as I write this book, Iraqi troops fight to reclaim the city of Mosul from ISIS control.

Oil has long played a role in history and in the world economy.

In 1941, Pearl Harbor was attacked after the United States cut off oil to Japan. The Vietnam War was about oil, not communism. The United States did not want China to have access to Vietnam's oil.

In my opinion, the Petrodollar must be defended. If oil is not traded in U.S. dollars, the U.S. economy collapses.

Three Giant Crashes

There have been three major crashes in the first 10 years of this century, between 2000 and 2010:

> 2000: the Dot-com Crash
> 2007: the Subprime Crash
> 2008: the Big Bank Crash

Three giant crashes—thousands of times bigger than the Giant Crash of 1929.

Many *Millionaires Next Door* were wiped out between 2000 and 2010. And many more are likely to be wiped out in the coming crash.

2002:

Rich Dad's Prophecy was published.

In 2002, *Rich Dad's Prophecy* was published. I predicted the biggest stock market crash would hit in or around 2016.

In that same book, I also predicted a smaller crash prior to 2016. That crash arrived in 2007 and 2008. (You can see my interview with CNN's Wolf Blitzer at: RichDad.com/TV

2008:

The third crash was the banking crash. Approximately six months later, on September 15, 2008, Lehman Brothers, a 150-year-old bank and one of the oldest banks in America, filed for bankruptcy and was closed.

On October 3, 2008, Ben Bernanke and Secretary of the Treasury Hank Paulson, a former Goldman Sachs CEO, created TARP, the

Troubled Assets Relief Program. The program bailed out the biggest banks—including Goldman Sachs, Paulson's former employer.

Taxpayers will be paying for this bailout for generations.

2009:

Muammar Gaddafi proposes selling Libyan oil in gold-backed dinars.

2011:

Gaddafi is killed.

2015:

Benjamin Netanyahu, the Prime Minister of Israel, is snubbed by President Barack Obama. Israel disagrees with President Obama's efforts to normalize relations with Iran.

Q: *Do you stand by your prediction of a crash in 2016?*
A: Yes.

In January 2016 the average investor lost 6.3% when the Dow plunged. The average NASDQ investor lost 8%. The crash was halted when the Fed and the Plunge Protection Team came to the rescue.

Oil prices have plunged. Interest rates have never, in the history of the world, been lower.

In August of 2016, it was reported that the mighty Deutsche Bank was in serious trouble. Steam was rising from its derivative portfolio. By the time you read this book, you will have a better idea of how pervasive this financial crisis is.

In *Rich Dad's Prophecy* (2002), I also predicted that terrorism would spread. One way to defeat America is to defeat the Petrodollar. If oil is not traded in dollars, the U.S. economy is in trouble.

In 2016, terrorist groups such as ISIS are growing.

In 2016, 60 Minutes, a television news magazine, does a story on the lawsuit filed against Saudi Arabia for attacking the United States.

In 2016, President Obama flies to Saudi Arabia to kiss the ring of the king.

Saudi Arabia and Iran are mortal enemies. Saudi Arabia is not happy with President Obama for lifting sanctions against Iran.

With low oil prices and Iran selling oil in Euros, Saudi Arabia's economy and social welfare programs are in trouble. Saudi Arabia is threatening to sell Aramco, its oil company, on the public market. The Saudis want their money now. They know the game is over.

China and Russia are building a pipeline and will trade oil in their currencies. The 1974 agreement that created the Petrodollar is coming apart.

The Crash

The facts tell the story. In 2016, millions of Americans have not had pay raises, cannot afford to buy a home, have little saved for retirement, and have children who are buried in student loan debt. At the same time, the U.S. government goes deeper and deeper into debt. For millions of people, their "giant crash" has already begun…

Not much has changed since 2007 and 2008. The problem only grows larger. And *that is the real problem.*

Q: *Didn't you feel sorry for the people who loss their homes?*

A: Yes. I hated seeing people lose their jobs, their houses, their retirement money, and their future. That is why I wrote *Rich Dad Poor Dad* in 1997 and *Rich Dad's Prophecy* in 2002. I was doing my best to warn people and to help them use financial education to prepare themselves. If it makes you feel better, we did not buy personal residences in foreclosure.

Q: *Are you saying the banks that caused the crash purchased the houses of those who lost their homes?*

A: In many cases, that was exactly what happened.

Another flashback…

It's January 2013. The organizations that purchased most of the personal residences were hedge funds and private equity funds, funded by Wall Street banks. Blackstone Group LP, the largest private real estate owner in the United States, accelerated purchases of single-family homes as prices jumped faster than expected.

According to Bloomberg.com, Blackstone has spent more than $2.5 billion on 16,000 homes to manage as rentals, deploying capital from a $13.3 billion fund. The firm is seeking to transform a market dominated by small investors into a new institutional asset class that JPMorgan Chase & Co. estimates could be worth as much as $1.5 trillion.

In late 2015, Blackstone announced it had stopped buying private residences as prices began rising again. The biggest real estate sale in history was over.

This is why crashes make the rich richer.

Q: *Are you saying the markets are rigged?*

A: Rather than answer your question specifically, I will tell you a story Warren Buffett told. He said, "If you are sitting at a poker table, and you do not know who the patsy is, you're the patsy."

Now do you understand why Bucky Fuller wrote *Grunch of Giants?* Now do you understand why this crisis could not have occurred if the Federal Reserve Bank and the IRS had not been first formed in 1913? Now do you understand, why there is no real financial education in our schools?

Now that you know how an idea of how to predict the future, what are you going to do?

When to Go Shopping

Everybody loves a bargain. Everyone knows the best time to go shopping is when the things you want are on sale.

Unfortunately most people shop for things that make them poorer, things like new flashy cars, new clothes, and jewelry.

The rich shop for bargains that make them richer. They wait for stock market crashes to buy the best stocks at bargain prices. They're poised for crashes so they can buy real estate at bargain prices. They buy gold and silver, and businesses, at bargain prices.

The rich do not invest for the long term or diversify and buy a little of everything... or buy anything that someone tells them to buy.

That is what Warren Buffett says about diversification:

> *"Diversification is protection against ignorance. It makes little sense if you know what you are doing."*

The problem with mutual funds is a mutual fund is already diversified, the same with an ETF and REIT. The same is true for a *fund of funds*.

Q: *What is a fund of funds?*

A: A fund of funds is a fund made up of other funds like mutual funds and ETFs, and REITs. It is diversification taken to the extreme.

All of these diversified products are created for the millionaire next door. Unfortunately, diversification does not protect you in a catastrophic crash, like the three crashes in the first of this century. In order to become a real investor in the I quadrant, you must learn to "cherry pick." You must learn to see what the financially blind cannot see.

Preparing for the Crash

Real financial education prepares you for a crash—before the crash hits.

Q: *How do you know when a crash is coming?*

A: There are many ways... and they include studying history, charts, reading, listening to wise men and women.

In my experience, the way you know a crash is imminent is when idiots become "investors."

For years, I knew a real estate crash was coming. The euphoria was growing. People with no income and no jobs were buying homes. My apartment houses were running high vacancies. Tenants who could not afford their rent were suddenly buying luxury homes. I knew the end was near when the cashier at the grocery store handed me her card and said, "Call me. I have some properties you may want to invest in." In an effort to seal the deal, she added: "Prices are going up, so act quickly."

The year was 2007. I thanked her and took her brand new business card. I knew the end was near and that soon it would be time to go shopping for bargains.

When to Buy

This was when Kim and I began buying real estate with partner and Rich Dad Advisor, Ken McElroy.

Chapter Six

WHY DEBT MAKES THE RICH RICHER

Poor Dad:
"Debt makes me poor."

Rich Dad:
"Debt makes me rich."

Debt is money.

One reason why the rich grow richer is because they use debt to become richer.

Unfortunately, without financial education, debt makes the poor and middle class poorer.

Donald Trump summed it up, saying: *"You know I am the king of debt. I love debt, but debt is tricky and it is dangerous."*

The housing market crashed when mortgage bankers began lending money to sub-prime borrowers, people who (in many cases) were without jobs and were encouraged to buy homes they could not afford.

Millions of middle class homeowners lost their homes when they began using their home as an ATM. Today, student loan debt is over $1.2 trillion—greater than all credit card debt.

It is the largest source of income for the U.S. government.

Although student loan debt makes the students who do not complete school poorer, student loan debt makes the U.S. government richer.

DÉJÀ VU

The Wall Street Journal • May 21, 2016

"U.S. credit card balances are on track to hit $1 trillion this year as banks aggressively push their plastic and consumers grow more comfortable carrying debt.

"That sum would come close to the all-time peak of $1.02 trillion set in July 2008, just before the financial crisis.

"In addition, lenders have signed up millions of subprime consumers who previously weren't able to get credit.

"Credit cards are one of the few business lines working for banks right now."

The Dollar Becomes Debt

In 1971, when President Nixon took the dollar off the gold standard, the dollar became debt. This was one of the biggest economic changes in world history.

In 1971, savers become losers—and debtors got rich.

How Debt Makes the Rich Richer

When I speak to groups around the world, I'm often asked this question: How does debt make the rich richer?

I will use credit cards as an example to illustrate this. Let's say you receive a new credit card. There is no money in that credit card. All you have is credit. You go shopping and buy a new pair of shoes that cost $100. You use your new credit card and—like magic—$100 of "money" has been created. At the same time $100 in debt has also been created. The $100 flows into the economy and people are happy. The problem is, you now have to work and pay off that $100 in debt.

Q: *So my ability to pay the $100 debt created the $100? My IOU, my promise, created the $100?*

A: Yes.

Q: *So the $100 is debt? A promise? Nothing more than an IOU from me?*

A: Yes.

Q: *Did I create that money out of nothing?*

A: Yes, in theory.

Q: *Is that why credit card companies are always offering me more and more credit cards?*

A: Exactly.

Q: *Why?*

A: There are many reasons.

One reason is that the economy grows when you and I create money by borrowing money. When you pay off your debt, the economy gets smaller.

Another reason is that debt makes the rich richer. If debt did not make the rich richer, the rich would not issue you a credit card.

The rich don't issue credit cards because they like you. They give you credit because they will make money, via interest, when you use your credit card. They'll make even more when you make only minimum payments on credit card balances.

Q: *So the government allows the rich to issue credit cards because the government needs the economy to grow and create jobs?*

A: Yes, in theory.

Like credit card holders, banks do not want countries to pay off their debts. Countries, like Greece, and the U.S. Territory of Puerto Rico, are facing *default*, which means they cannot make the "minimum" interest payments on their debt. The banks will allow a country to "restructure" their debt. *Restructure* means they will allow the country to refinance its debt, which means banks will lend them *more* money, which enables them to continue to make interest payments.

Q: *The banks will actually lend a country more money… so they can make their "minimum payments?"*

A: Yes. They will and they do.

Q: *Is that why the credit card companies only ask for a minimum payment? So I never pay off the debt?*

A: Yes. Your minimum credit card payment is like a renter paying rent. You never pay off your credit card debt and the renter never owns the home or apartment he or she lives in. Your minimum monthly credit card payment makes the rich richer in the same way monthly rental payments make real estate investors richer.

Money for Nothing

In the example of the credit card and new shoes, the $100 was created out of nothing. The moment the credit card was used, the $100 of debt became an *asset* for the rich and the same $100 became a liability for the poor and middle class credit card holder.

Q: *So if I want to be rich, I need to learn to use debt to get rich?*

A: Yes, in theory. You must be very careful with debt. It takes financial education to learn how to use debt to get rich.

Debt is a double-edged sword. Debt can make you rich and then, suddenly, something changes and that same debt is making you poor, very poor.

That is what happened when the real estate market began to crash in 2007. Millions of people thought they were rich because they had equity in their homes—equity that many people had used as their personal ATMs. And then, suddenly, the market crashed and they were upside down. They've owed more on their home than it was worth. Overnight, they were *poor.* Many lost everything.

That is why Kim and I created the *CASHFLOW* board game. It is the only financial education game that encourages players to use debt to win the game.

Q: *Learning to use debt with play money before using real money?*

A: Exactly. But don't ever forget: Debt can be dangerous. Debt is like a loaded gun. A loaded gun can save your life—but it can also kill you.

Financial Fools

When I say, "I use debt to buy *assets*," many people say, "That is risky." Yet those same people have no problem using a credit card to buy *liabilities,* such as a pair of $100 shoes.

Rich Debtors

Apple, one of the richest companies in the world, has approximately $246 billion sitting in the bank. Yet it has borrowed billions of dollars over the past few years because of low interest rates. Why does Apple borrow? Apple borrows because debt is cheaper than repatriating cash, which means bringing money back into the country and paying U.S. taxes on it.

Rich CEOs

Many corporate executives are paid in *stock options* rather than money. This causes CEOs to borrow money and buy back their company shares. When the share price goes up, the CEOs and executives sell their "options" at high prices, making them richer... but making the company employees and shareholders poorer.

Since the 1970s, many CEOs have been using debt to speculate in the stock market rather than use debt to grow the company and create more jobs.

Learning to Use Debt

So, how does a person learn to use debt as money? I'll start with a story you may have heard before.

In 1973, the year I returned to Hawaii from Vietnam, my poor dad suggested I go to graduate school to get my MBA. My rich dad suggested I learn to invest in real estate.

My poor dad encouraged me to become a high-paid employee in the E quadrant. My rich dad encouraged me to be a professional investor in the I quadrant.

While watching television one day, an infomercial came on advertising a free seminar on investing in real estate. I attended the free seminar, liked what I heard, and invested $385 for a three-day course. That $385 was a lot of money at the time, because I was still in the Marine Corps and not making much money.

The three-day program was great. The instructor was real—a rich, experienced, and successful investor who loved to teach. I learned a lot from him. At the end of the program, the instructor gave me some of the best advice I have ever received. He said, "Your education begins when you leave the class."

His assignment was for all of us to get together in groups of three to five students to look at and write an evaluation of 100 properties that were for sale. He gave us 90 days to complete the assignment. He didn't want us to buy anything, or invest any money, for at least 90 days.

Initially, there were five people in our group. By the first meeting, we were down to three or four. By the end of the 90 days, our group was down to two.

Back to School

After 90 days of looking at and writing one-page evaluations on 100 properties, I identified my first real estate investment opportunity. It was a 1-bedroom/1-bath condominium, next to the beach on the island of Maui. The entire development was in foreclosure and the price for the condo was $18,000. The seller was offering 90% financing.

All I had to do was come up with $1,800 for a 10% down payment. I handed the real estate broker my credit card for the down payment and the property was mine. I purchased my first investment property with 100% OPM—Other People's Money. I had none of my own money in the investment.

At the end of every month, after all the expenses were paid, including debt service and management fees, the property put approximately $25 in my pocket, an *infinite return* on my investment. It was an infinite return because I didn't have any of my own money in the deal.

While $25 a month is not a lot of money, the lessons learned have proven to be priceless. One of the lessons learned was that *debt is money* and the other lesson was *debt is tax-free*.

Q: *Why is debt tax-free?*

A: Two very important words in financial literacy are *debt* and *equity*. In simple terms, *equity* is your money. *Debt* is OPM, other people's money.

When a person buys a property, they generally start the process with a *down payment*. In most cases that down payment, the owner's equity, is made with after-tax dollars. The owner has already paid the income tax on that money.

Q: *When you used debt as a down payment, there was no income tax to pay?*

A: Correct. Debt can be very inexpensive money if you know how to use it to make money. Debt is extremely expensive if you use debt to buy liabilities (such as that pair of shoes) with a credit card and make only minimum payments.

Q: *So your first real estate investment was made with 100% debt and you made $25 net cash flow income every month?*

A: Yes. And that $25 net cash flow income was also tax-free.

Q: *How did you do that?*

A: That is what financial education is for. Tom Wheelwright, CPA and my tax advisor, explained taxes and tax strategies in the previous chapter—Why Taxes Make the Rich Richer.

Tax Lessons from Tom

Why Debt Is Tax Free

The general rule is that all income is taxable. Income is money you receive that is yours to spend as you please with no strings attached. Debt is not income. You have to pay it back. So when you borrow money for an investment, it's really tax-free money. This makes debt less expensive than equity. Equity is your money that has already been taxed. So even if you have a 5-6% interest rate, the debt is far cheaper than if you had to use equity on which you paid 40% tax.

Advanced Strategies

Obviously, the $18,000 property on the island of Maui is an overly simplified example. Today, that same property is worth approximately $300,000. And I wish I hadn't sold it!

Kim's first real estate investment was $45,000. She put down $5,000 and made $50 a month in positive cash flow.

The deal: The bank allowed Kim to "assume" the seller's debt. The bank did not want the house—it wanted the monthly payments from the mortgage holder. Two years later, Kim sold the house for $90,000 and reinvested her *capital gains* into additional investment properties.

Today, Kim and I, along with Rich Dad Advisor Ken McElroy, own approximately 10,000 rental units. We have cash flow, tax-free, every month without working, and earn more money than many people earn in a lifetime. The real estate investment process is the same, the only thing that has changed are the number of zeros on the checks we deposit.

What has increased over the years is our financial education and experience.

I feel for people who, like Pavlov's dogs, simply do what they are told or what they're conditioned to do, mindlessly handing their money over to Wall Street, investing for the long term… and learning nothing.

This is a very big reason why the rich are getting richer.

Q: *Isn't using your credit card, debt, for your down payment risky?*

A: Yes, but much less risky than buying $1,800 worth of shoes. Real estate generally holds its value. Shoes lose 90% to 100% of their value the moment you wear them. Who wants to rent shoes? Many people love renting a nice condo on a white-sand beach in Hawaii.

INCOME STATEMENT

Income
Expenses Debt – *poor people use* *credit card for living* *expenses (food, clothes, gas)*

BALANCE SHEET

Assets	Liabilities
Debt – *rich* *people use debt* *to buy assets*	Debt – *the* *middle class* *uses debt to buy* *liabilities (like a* *house and cars)*

This is yet another reason why the rich are getting richer. The rich focus on assets more than income and they use debt to acquire and grow those assets.

In the *CASHFLOW* game, there are Big Deals and Small Deals. It's interesting to observe people as they play the game. I've found that you can always spot a loser, just by watching behavior. The loser always starts with the Big Deals.

Bankers Love Real Estate

There are four basic asset classes. They are:

1. Businesses
2. Real estate
3. Paper Assets: Stocks and Bonds
4. Commodities

It is possible to secure financing, debt, in all four asset classes. Of the four, real estate is the easiest. Bankers love lending money on real estate. And there are good reasons for that.

Business Loans

If you went to your banker and said, "I want to borrow a million dollars to start a business," the banker may not talk to you. If they are accommodating, they may recommend that you apply for a SBA loan, a loan from the Small Business Administration. If you do not own real estate, it is not easy getting a business loan.

Tax Lessons from Tom

Banks Want Security

One reason a bank is less likely to loan for a business start-up is because banks like security. Real estate is secure. The bank knows the real estate will likely hold its value. So if you don't pay the loan back, the bank has the security of taking over the property and getting paid by selling the property. The bank could not sell your business if it fails. So there is very little security for the bank in a business loan. That's why the bank wants the SBA to guarantee the loan–so the bank gets paid if your business fails.

Loans for Stocks and Bonds

A stockbroker may let you invest in stocks and bonds *on margin*, which means you have some *credit* or credit line with the broker. If you make a mistake and lose money, the stockbroker will immediately issue a *margin call*, and sell whatever assets you have put up as collateral.

Tax Lessons from Tom

Margin Loans

Stocks are very liquid so they do represent pretty good security for a loan. However, they move up and down very quickly. That's why the broker will only lend you a small portion (normally not more than 50%) of the value of your stock portfolio. They need to be able to liquidate it quickly if you don't pay it back or if the stocks lose value.

Commodity Loans

If you plan on buying gold or silver with debt, I doubt many bankers will lend you anything. The bank may hold gold and silver as *collateral* but I have yet to have a banker lend me a million dollars at 5% interest for 15 years... to buy gold or silver.

Gold and silver coins have legs. Real estate does not move. Governments keep years of documents, legal descriptions, historical chain of ownership, and how the property was bought and sold. These are just a few reasons why bankers love real estate.

If you are going into business or investing in real estate, investing in financial education first, then starting small to gain real life experience is essential.

The good news is: You can get rich in all four asset classes—if you are financially educated.

Choose Your Quadrants Wisely

> Q: *Is that why your rich dad advised you to take a real estate investment class before you got out of the Marine Corps?*
>
> A: That was one reason. His main reason was to have me focus on the I quadrant early in my life.

My poor dad wanted me to focus on finding a high paying job in the E quadrant.

There are many ways to get to real estate heaven. *The Real Book of Real Estate* is a collection of strategies and formulas written by real, real estate investors. In that book, two of Donald Trump's sons, Don Jr. and Eric, share what they have learned from their father.

Once Upon a Time

Once upon a time... governments would pay you interest income to encourage you to buy their bonds, bonds issued to pay for a government that was living beyond its means, and spending more than it collected in tax revenue.

Once upon a time... banks would compete for your savings. Banks would offer free toasters and steak knives—even cash—to encourage you to deposit your money with them.

Today, a growing number of banks in Europe, the United States and Asia are actively discouraging deposits. Today Europe and Japan are charging savers to save money. It is known as NIRP, negative interest rate policy. It's just a matter of time before the rest of the world follows suit. It's proof positive that savers have become losers.

What does this mean? It means the world has too much money. Bankers do not want your savings because your savings are the bank's liability. The banks want debtors, people who know how to borrow money. That is why interest rates are so low.

Once upon a time... people trusted bankers to channel their savings into productive projects, growing the economy.

Today, bankers and corporate executives are not reinvesting savers' money to grow the economy.

I dropped out of the MBA program after six months. Rather than learn how to grow a business, which is what I had expected, I was learning how to "make a lot of money manipulating the markets."

Today, our business schools continue to teach our best and brightest students how to make a lot of money manipulating the markets, rather than teaching how to invest in research and development, grow their businesses, and create jobs.

The stock market and banks were created to help companies raise money to grow their businesses and for savers and investors to grow with the company. It is the ultimate irony that our richest companies are actively involved in borrowing money from banks and investing in the stock market when they do not need money.

This is another reason why the poor and middle class grow poorer.

Finally, the American public is realizing how deeply and profoundly broken the economy is, and the extent to which it is not working for the majority of American people.

This is why Senator Bernie Sanders' campaign cry was:

> *"The issue of wealth and income inequality is the great moral issue of our time."*

That moral crisis begins in our schools. Our schools, K-12, teach little to nothing about money. Most people still believe in saving money, not realizing that after 1971 debt is money. Without financial education, most people do not realize that the rules of money have changed.

If you want to grow richer, invest in your financial education before you practice using debt as money. Learning to use debt to make you rich gives you unbelievable power, a power very few will ever experience.

SUMMARY

The gap between the rich and the poor is caused by these things:

1. Financial advisors
2. Taxes
3. Debt
4. Mistakes
5. Saving money
6. Crashes

Now that you have completed Part One you are better able to see both sides of the same coin. I trust you can see that the way to the other side of the coin is through real financial education.

But before going into financial education, it is very important to understand what financial education is *not*, as well as the price of financial illiteracy in your life.

Part Two

WHAT FINANCIAL EDUCATION IS NOT

Introduction to Part Two

A TALE OF
TWO TEACHERS

Many people believe they are financially educated. As you read this book, I am sure you will gain a better understanding about where you fall on the financial education spectrum. You may find that you agree with my rich dad and decide that you have a lot to learn about money and investing.

Before continuing with "What financial education is…" I think it makes sense to cover what financial education *isn't*.

For example, most people believe their house is an *asset*. Yet, in most cases, their house is really a *liability*. Labeling a *liability* an *asset* is one of the main reasons there is a growing gap between the rich and everyone else.

Financially Il-literacy

After defining what financial education is not, the next chapter goes into financial literacy and, more importantly, what will happen to people who are financially il-literate, when the economy changes again.

So if you are ready to find out how solid your *financial education* is and how *financially literate* you are, you're ready for Part Two.

Chapter Seven

WHAT FINANCIAL EDUCATION IS... NOT

Poor Dad:

*"Why do I need financial education? I have a great education.
I have a great job. I have a house, money in the bank,
and a government retirement."*

Rich Dad:

"If you argue with an idiot, there are two idiots."

There is financial education for the poor and middle class. And, on the other side of the coin, there is financial education for the rich.

This is why Warren Buffett said:

> *"Wall Street is the only place that people ride to in a Rolls Royce to get advice from those who take the subway."*

Before getting into what *real financial education* is, it is important to discuss the other side of the coin, what *financial education is not.*

What Financial Education Is Not

Rich Dad Poor Dad was published in 1997 and made *The New York Times* best-sellers list in the year 2000.

Soon after making that prestigious list, I was a guest on *Oprah!* and interviewed by Oprah Winfrey. In one hour I went from unknown to almost famous.

The phones began ringing and I was soon a frequent guest on numerous television shows, radio programs and interviewed for magazines and newspapers around the world. Most interviews were about the story of my two dads—one rich and one poor. No one asked me about financial education.

Almost every person who interviewed me was educated and was certain they knew what financial education was.

As rich dad says, *"If you argue with an idiot, there are two idiots."* It was a test of diplomacy to explain that *their idea* of financial education was not the same as my rich dad's ideas on financial education. We were not on the same side of the same coin.

The following are examples of what highly-educated people believe financial education is:

> **Economics:** Many journalists thought *economics* was financial education. While the understanding of economics is important, economics was not my rich dad's idea of financial education. Rich dad often said, "If the study of economics made you rich, why are most economists poor?"
>
> Today, the U.S. Federal Reserve Bank employs more economists with PhDs than any other institution. If economists with PhDs could make us rich, why is the U.S. economy in trouble? Just look at the chart on the following page:

U.S. National Debt

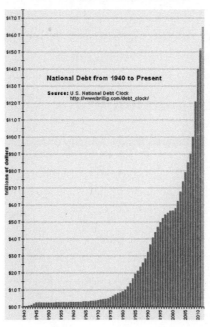

Source: National Debt Clock

You do not need a PhD in economics to know that those economists are being paid too much.

Balancing a checkbook: During an interview, a famous American TV host said, "Financial education is knowing how to balance a checkbook." When I disagreed with him, he cut me off and went on to another subject.

Balancing a checkbook is important. But my mom and dad could balance a checkbook, and they were still poor.

Saving money: Every interviewer believed that saving money was intelligent, the smart thing to do.

Most interviewers cringed when I said, *"Savers are losers."*

A real financial education must include the history of money. Most interviewers were not aware that in 1971, the year President Nixon took the dollar off the gold standard, the United States and the world began printing money.

Why would an intelligent person save money when governments are printing money?

Here are two charts we've looked at earlier in this book to reinforce what happens when governments print money.

The Fed's Expansion of the Monetary Base

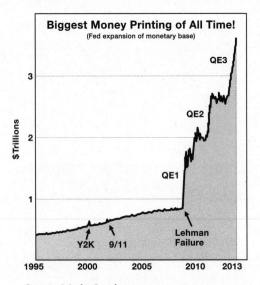

Source: MarketInsider

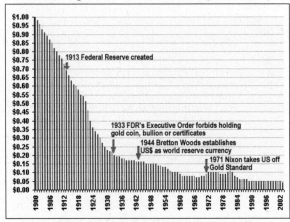

Source: http://eh.net/hmit/ppowerusd/

A financially-educated person knows that when banks and governments are printing money, the value of money is going down and the cost of living is going up.

As you know, *"It's the money, stupid."*

Knowing your FICO score: A FICO® score is a particular brand of credit score. A credit score is a number that is used to predict how likely you are to pay back a loan on time. Credit scores are used by companies to make decisions on credit worthiness, on whether or not to offer you a mortgage, a loan, or a credit card.

Your credit score is important, but it is not financial education. Many poor and middle class people have great credit scores.

Getting out of debt: My poor dad believed debt was bad. He believed in "living debt free." Given his limited financial education, living debt free was a good idea. Living debt free is good advice for the poor and middle class.

Rich dad often said, "Debt is money." He also said, "There is good debt and bad debt. Good debt makes you rich and bad debt makes you poor. If you want to use debt to get rich, you must invest in your financial education to understand the difference between good debt and bad debt, And how to use debt." Below is a picture of the banking system.

True financial education must explain the big picture of the banking system. The banking system is a system of savers and debtors. As the illustration on the previous page shows, *without debtors, the money system of the world would collapse.*

This is why most bank credit cards offer free travel, or cash back, and other "perks," to encourage people to get into debt. The banks make money from debtors, not savers. After the 2007 real estate mortgage crash, credit cards became the number-one source of income for many banks.

Poor dad used debt to buy his house and car. That's bad debt. Bad debt buys liabilities. Bad debt is debt you have to pay for.

Rich dad used debt to buy investment properties and grow his business. That's good debt, and good debt makes you richer. Good debt is debt someone else pays for. Governments give tax breaks to people who know how to use good debt.

The world banking system is built on the Fractional Reserve Banking System. This means that for every dollar a saver puts in the bank, the bank can lend a multiple of that dollar to debtors. For example, if the fractional reserve is 10, that means the bank can lend $10 for every $1 a saver deposits. If inflation is too high, the Central Bank (such as the Federal Reserve in the United States) can use its tools to effectively lower the fraction a bank can lend to, let's say, 5... with only $5 dollars available to the bank to lend for every $1 deposited by a saver.

When banks lower interest rates as they are doing today, they are saying, "We do not want savers. We want debtors."

Low interest rates on savings are forcing the middle class into the stock market and real estate markets, hoping for a better return on their money. The middle classes is chasing "bubbles" in financial markets. If the bubbles burst, many in the middle class may lose everything.

Low interest rates mean send this message: "Please come and borrow money. Money is on sale."

For the rich, low interest rates make it easier to get richer. For the poor and middle class, especially savers, low interest rates spell financial disaster.

Ironically, *savings are taxed* and *debt is tax-free money*. Which is another reason for the rich getting richer.

Tax Lessons from Tom

Savings and Debt Are Opposite Sides of the Tax Coin

Not only is interest on savings and debt taxed differently—savings is taxed and debt is not—the interest paid on good debt (debt used to buy assets) is deductible. So debt actually lowers your taxes while savings increase your taxes.

Living below your means: Once upon a time, living below your means and saving money made sense. You could achieve financial security, possibly even become rich, by living frugally and saving for your future.

After 1971, the year President Nixon took the dollar off the gold standard and opened the doors for the banks and government to print money, living below your means and saving money made *no sense*.

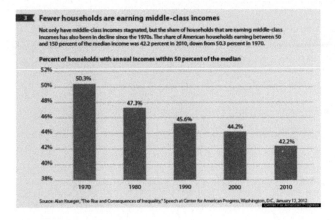

Source: Alan Krueger

The chart on the preceding page tells the story of what is happening to the middle class. Living below your means and saving money is not financially intelligent.

Today, living below your means only makes the poor and middle class poorer.

Investing for the long term: Let's look again at the graph below that shows what has been happening over the last 120 years in the stock market. As you can see, "investing for the long term" made sense from 1895 to 2000.

120 Years of the Dow

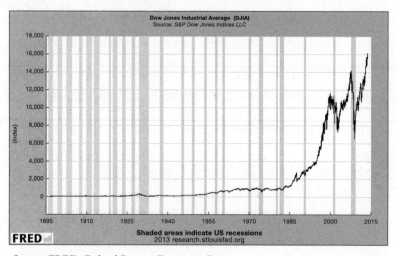

Source: FRED–Federal Reserve Economic Data

Between 2000 and 2010 the world has experienced three major crashes. In 2000, we witnessed the dot.com crash. In 2007, it was the subprime real estate crash. And in 2008, was the banking crash.

As you saw in the chart of Warren Buffett's company in Chapter 1— it's proof that even the greatest investor in the world could not prevent his company, Berkshire Hathaway, from losing money after 2000.

I believe bigger crashes are coming.

Many people say, "Don't worry. Nothing will be as big as the giant crash in 1929." I'm not one of them.

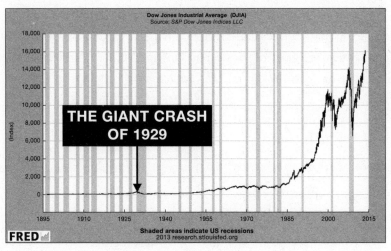

Source: FRED—Federal Reserve Economic Data

So I ask you: Why invest for the long term if the next crash will be thousands of times bigger than the giant crash of 1929?

In 2002, the book *Rich Dad's Prophecy* was published. It predicted that the biggest crash of all time was likely to occur in 2016... plus or minus a few years. The next chart asks an important question: What's next?

What's Next?

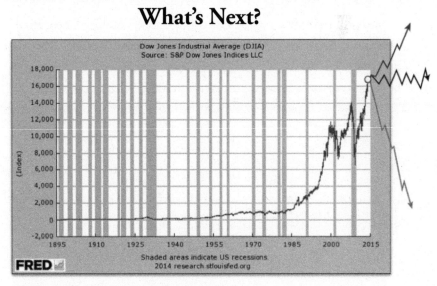

Source: FRED—Federal Reserve Economic Data

If the markets keep going up, investing for the long term makes sense. If the market does crash, the rich will get richer. On the flip side, unfortunately, millions of people will be wiped out. If you want to get richer, you may want to stop taking advice from people who ride the subway.

How Bad Can It Get?

Well...

Q: *Is it possible someone will stop the insanity and save the world economy?*

A: Anything is possible. The problem is the world economy is a house of cards.

Q: *How fast could the economy come down?*

A: If it does collapse, the economy will probably come down in stages, which means you will have time to change with the changes, if you are prepared.

A book I recommend to everyone who is interested in the future of the global economy is *When Money Destroys Nations* by Philip Haslam. It is a great, financially accurate book, and easy to read and understand.

Philip Haslam is a very bright young man, a qualified chartered accountant, economic advisor, author, and speaker. He lives in Johannesburg, South Africa. When Tom and I are in South Africa, Philip joins us on stage, supporting Tom Wheelwright on South African tax law, the consequences of printing money, bitcoin, and the global economy.

Living in South Africa, Philip decided to cross the border into Zimbabwe to witness, firsthand, a modern-day financial collapse of a once extremely rich country—a collapse due not to war or natural disaster, but to the unrestrained printing of money.

The Six Gorges

In his book, Philip explains "the six gorge moments of hyperinflation." In his South Africa, there is a deep ravine cut into the mountains and interspersed with six perilous waterfalls, known as Suicide Gorge. He describes leaping from the first cliff to a deep pool below. Looking back, he realized there was only one way out. He had to keep jumping, leaping off ever larger, surging waterfalls, into smaller shallower pools.

He uses his experience of Suicide Gorge as a metaphor to explain a six-step financial collapse.

He tells the story of Zimbabwe's six-step collapse through the eyes of the people who actually went through the collapse. The stories are disturbing. If you want some motivation to do something now, please read his book.

The following are excerpts from Philip's book, statements from people who lived through the collapse.

> *"They eventually had to sell their home, which kept them alive for three years. After that, he and his wife became destitute and had to move to South Africa to live with their son. Two years later, they both died."*
>
> *"My dad's friend was a partner at a legal firm, having worked there for 50 years. For that entire period he had invested his retirement savings with Old Mutual (the investment company for employees). With hyperinflation, his retirement savings were decimated. Old Mutual sent him a letter saying it wasn't worth paying him monthly so they paid out the entire amount. With that payment—his entire life's pension—he bought a jerrycan of fuel."*
>
> *"How can you take money that is losing value? You can't. The government was forcing us to use the paper money."*
>
> *"The pantry was kept under lock and key because food was our equivalent currency; it was our investment and savings. We could buy anything with our food—labour, sugar, rice, fuel, etc. It was our money."*

"In women's prisons, there were shortage of tampons and sanitary pads. The demand for these was higher than U.S. dollars, and sanity products soon circulated as a medium of exchange in these prison."

"Hyperinflation made everyone a criminal because you had to break the law to survive."

"An elderly lady who worked for us part-time went to buy books for the orphans we helped. She purchased a stack of books and paid the bookseller in U.S. dollars. Just then an undercover government agent pounced. We were forced to pay a bribe. I hate bribes, but when the choice is watching an elderly lady go to jail or paying a bribe, you pay the bribe."

"Their lives petered out to a withered end. They couldn't get any medication, food, or water and few understood why their money couldn't buy anything. There were many stories of pensioners dying in their homes and many elderly couples quietly ending their lives together as they reached rock bottom."

Once a Rich Country

Many people say, "That happened in Zimbabwe because Zimbabwe is a poor country." I remind them that less than 50 years ago, Zimbabwe was a very rich country, known as "the bread basket of Africa."

Today, Venezuela is in the same condition as Zimbabwe. Venezuela is also a very rich country, with the largest oil reserves in the world. So the question is, how did people in once-rich countries allow this to happen to them?

Philip's book tells the story:

*"As inflation increased, Zimbabweans lost confidence in Zimbabwe dollars, the government resorted to extensive control measures, it managed prices, fiddled with inflation rates, and **used obscure language that made it difficult to understand definitively what was going on.**"*

Fed-Speak

Alan Greenspan, former Federal Reserve Bank Chairman (1987 to 2006), is famous for Fed Speak. These are Greenspan's own words:

> *"Since becoming a central banker, I have learned to mumble with great incoherence. If I seem unduly clear to you, you must have misunderstood what I said."*

Listening to Fed Speak, or to any central banker, is definitely, not financial education. It is financial misinformation. If Fed Chairman Greenspan, Ben Bernanke, and now Janet Yellen were honest, they would simply say, *"It's the money, stupid."*

I asked Philip Haslam what gorge he thought the world was jumping into in 2016. His answer, "I believe gorge #3, possibly gorge #4."

Now you have a general idea what financial education is not, the next chapter will explain the price of being financially illiterate.

Chapter Eight

ARE YOU FINANCIALLY ILLITERATE?

Poor Dad:
"My house is an asset."

Rich Dad:
"My house is a liability."

My poor dad was a highly-educated man. He was class valedictorian, graduated from college in two years, and went on to study at Stanford, the University of Chicago, and Northwestern University, ultimately earning his PhD.

Unfortunately, he was not financially literate. He did not know the difference between *assets* and *liabilities* because he did not speak the language of money.

His *financial illiteracy* required him to work harder—although he never got ahead financially. Every year he received a pay raise, but his expenses also increased. He did his best to manage his money, but money seemed to slip through his fingers.

Although he was a highly-educated, honest, hard-working family man with four kids—and a pillar of the community—he died a poor man.

The Price of Illiteracy

We all know the importance of literacy, the ability to read, write, speak, and do basic math. Literacy is a human being's connection to the outside world.

The following are five statistics on illiteracy.

1. Two-thirds of students who cannot read proficiently by the end of 4th grade will end up in jail or on welfare.

2. Over 70% of America's prison inmates cannot read above a 4th grade level.

3. One in four children in America grow up without learning how to read.

4. Students who don't read proficiently by the 3rd grade are four times more likely to drop out of school.

5. As of 2011, America was the only free-market OECD (Organization for Economic Cooperation and Development) country in which the current generation was less educated than the previous one.

The Price of Financial Il-literacy

I'm sure you'll agree that the price we pay for a lack of financial education is a high one.

Financial illiteracy immobilizes people. Financially illiterate people live in fear, clinging to a false sense of security. Fear keeps people poor. Financially illiterate people cannot solve life's basic financial problems.

Financial illiteracy destroys self-esteem. Without financial literacy, a person's self-respect and self-worth are often low, rendering them unable to act effectively and decisively. A financially illiterate person goes through life pretending he or she knows what they are doing with money.

Financial illiteracy causes people to be frustrated and upset.
The number one reason for divorce is arguments over money.
Financially illiterate people cannot find the right answers to solve
their money problems. Always worried about not having enough
money, many are unable to live happy, prosperous, fulfilling lives.

Financially illiterate people create fixed ideas. I've found that
financially illiterate people have closed minds. Many believe the
rich are evil, greedy, and cruel. Many believe more money will solve
their problems.

Financially illiterate people often say, *"You can't do that here."* They
persist in this belief, even if financially literate people are doing it—
right in front of them. Their financial illiteracy limits lives. Fixed
ideas block out the pain, confusion, stupidity, and helplessness that
result from a lack of education.

Financially illiterate people believe they are victims. Without
financial literacy a person does not know what is going on in
the world economy. They tend to blame others for their money
problems. Many blame the rich for their money problems.

Most people are victims of the tax system. When they hear the
rich pay little to nothing in taxes, they get angry. Rather than find
out *how* the rich pay less in taxes (or how they could minimize the
taxes they themselves pay) they call the rich "crooks and cheats."

Financial illiteracy causes blindness. Financially illiterate people
cannot see the millions of dollars in opportunities... right in front
of them.

Financially illiterate people trust strangers they have never met with
their money more than they trust themselves. That is why millions
of people ask, "What should I do with my money?" and then invest
for the long term, without ever really knowing who is "managing"
their money.

Financially illiterate people cannot see market crashes coming and
operate on trust.

Financial illiteracy causes poverty. The irony is that, in a world awash with money, the middle class is shrinking and poverty is rising.

Even though the banks have printed trillions of dollars, billions of people continue to say, "I can't afford it." And although interest rates are at all-time lows, billions of people still cannot get a loan or afford to buy a home.

Financially illiterate people make poor investors. Financially illiterate people are in the wrong place at the wrong time and usually invest in the wrong things at the wrong time for the wrong reasons. They buy high and sell low. When Walmart has a sale, they rush in and buy. When Wall Street has a sale, they run away from the best investments, investments that are "on sale" at low prices.

Financial illiteracy causes poor judgment. A financially illiterate person does not understand value. Often this person buys cheap, rather than paying for quality. A financially illiterate person cannot comprehend what is important, what is valuable, what needs to be done, or the consequences of their actions.

Financial illiteracy causes a person to hate life. Millions are stuck in jobs they hate, not earning the money they want and need to earn. It is estimated that 70% of all American workers actually hate their jobs. They sell their most valuable asset, their life, for a paycheck.

Financial illiteracy can lead to unethical actions. Financial illiteracy erodes moral, ethical, and legal values. We've all heard horror stories of people who start "dealing" or "hooking" or "gambling" just to make a little money on the side.

Millions cheat, lie, and steal for money. Many people would cheat on their taxes, rather than learn how to reduce their taxes legally.

Tax Lessons from Tom

Tax Cheating Around the World

Several times each year, I will run into someone who wants me to help them cheat on their taxes–or at least condone their cheating. Each time, I explain that when you understand the tax law you don't have to cheat. Some people will listen and learn and stop cheating. Others will continue to cheat because they are too lazy to do it the right way. In Italy, the tax law actually refers to two levels of tax cheats. Minor tax cheating has one penalty and major tax cheating has a different penalty. As we travel, Robert and I encounter people in countries where it is the norm for people to cheat on their taxes. This doesn't have to happen. With financial education, anyone can pay less tax legally and never have to fear that the tax collector will catch them cheating.

Financial illiteracy distorts reality. When people are stressed and anxious because they are financially strapped, they don't always have a clear view of reality. They don't always see the options and opportunities open to them. For example, many believe a big home, flashy car, nice clothes, expensive wines, and bling make them rich.

Step by Step

As with many things in life, financial education is a process:

Financial education improves financial literacy;

Financial literacy increases a person's ability to solve financial problems;

Solving financial problems makes the person financially smarter;

And a financially smarter person is a richer person.

Q: *Are you saying the more money problems I solve the richer I become?*

A: Yes. A rich person can usually solve financial problems the poor and middle class cannot.

Q: *And are you saying that if I avoid solving my money problems I become poorer?*

A: Yes. And if you do not solve your problems, they pile up like unpaid bills… which leads to bigger problems.

Q: *Isn't our government doing the same thing?*

A: It is.

Q: *So how do we change the world?*

A: That's the question, isn't it? My rich dad often said: "If you want to change the world, start by changing yourself." Whenever I was complaining and whining about something, he would have me repeat to myself:

"For things to change… first I must change."

What Is Financial Literacy?

One of rich dad's most important lessons was:

"How you solve your problems determines the rest of your life."

In 1997, *Rich Dad Poor Dad* was published. It is a book on financial literacy, about nine-year-old boys… rich dad's son and me. For those who have read *Rich Dad Poor Dad*, this will be a review… with a few embellishments.

The Financial Statement

Pictured on the following page is the simple diagram rich dad used to develop our financial literacy. It is rich dad's version of a financial statement.

This simple diagram changed the direction of my life. If not for this simple way to visualize and understand income and expenses and assets and liabilities, I might have followed in my poor dad's footsteps and become an employee who worked hard, and struggled with money all my life.

INCOME STATEMENT

Income
Expenses

BALANCE SHEET

Assets	Liabilities

The financial statement is at the core of financial literacy. That is why rich dad often said, "My banker never asks me for my report card. My banker does not care what school I went to or my grade point average. My banker wants to see my financial statement. Your financial statement is your report card after you leave school."

Financial literacy—the basics, at a young age—gave me a clearer direction for my life.

People who cannot read financial statements are *financially illiterate.* As you know, there are many highly-educated people that cannot read financial statements. This is the real financial crisis we face.

Pictures Not Words

Since rich dad's son and I were only nine years old when our financial education began, rich dad used pictures and very few words. Today, as a grown man, I still prefer using pictures and very few words.

INCOME STATEMENT

Income
Poor Dad focused here
Expenses

BALANCE SHEET

Assets	Liabilities
Rich Dad focused here	

My poor dad worked for job security and a steady paycheck. Rich dad worked for assets that produced cash flow. Which column are you focused on... Income or Assets?

Tax Lessons from Tom

The Power of Financial Statements

I can tell a person's financial literacy by looking at which financial statements they use and how they use them. Employees tend to look only at income. On a tax return, employees only have to report their income. Very few of their expenses are deductible. So for employees, those in the E quadrant, their pay stub is their financial statement.

Small business owners tend to look at income and expense. This is the income statement. It tells the story of what money they earned and what they spent. On a tax return, small business owners only have to report their income and expenses. They are not required to have a balance sheet. So for small business owners, those in the S quadrant, the profit and loss, or income statement is the only financial statement they use.

Those in the B and the I quadrants use at least two more financial statements. They use a balance sheet, which reports their assets and liabilities, and they use a statement of cash flows, which shows where their cash came from and where it went. On a tax return, big business owners and professional investors are required to show their income statement and their balance sheet. They are expected to show their statement of cash flows to their banker along with their income statement and balance sheet.

When we prepare tax returns at my CPA firm, we require all of our business and investment clients, no matter how large or small, to prepare both an income statement and a balance sheet. This way, we have much greater assurance that the information they are providing is accurate. Tax collectors feel the same way. A business is five times more likely to be audited if they only show their income statement on their tax return than if they also show their balance sheet.

Six Important Words

There are six words at the core of financial literacy. They are:

1. Income
2. Expense
3. Assets
4. Liabilities
5. Cash
6. Flow

Ask any entrepreneur what the two most important words are, and they will say *cash flow*.

Q: *Why are cash and flow the two most important words?*

A: Because *cash* and *flow* determine if something is income, expense, asset, or liability.

For example, ***income*** *is cash flowing in. An* ***expense*** *is cash flowing out.*

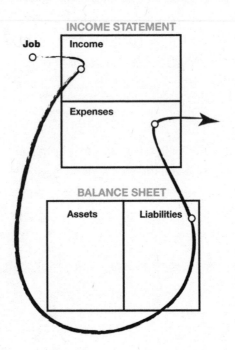

In the real world, this might be a checkbook—*income in* and *expenses out.*

> Q: *Is that why you say balancing a checkbook is not really financial education?*
>
> A: Exactly.

> Q: *Because a checkbook does not include assets and liabilities?*
>
> A: Exactly. My mom and dad balanced their checkbook, but had no idea what *assets* or liabilities were. That is why they were poor.

Every month they would wonder where their money went. Their money was flowing out via *liabilities,* such as their house and car... *liabilities* they were calling *assets.*

> Q: *So assets and liabilities determine if someone is rich, poor, or middle class?*
>
> A: Yes. The different classes focus on different columns in the financial statement, as pictured below.

INCOME STATEMENT

Income
Expenses
The poor

BALANCE SHEET

Assets	Liabilities
The rich	The middle class

Q: *Are you saying the poor are always trying to save money by reducing expenses?*

A: Yes.

Q: *And the rich focus on assets?*

A: Yes.

Q: *So why does the middle class focus on liabilities.*

A: Because, in most cases, they do not know the difference between *assets* and *liabilities.*

Q: *Is that why your poor dad called his house an asset? And rich dad called his house a liability?*

A: Yes.

Q: *Why was that?*

A: The answer is financial literacy. And, the other side of the coin: financial illiteracy.

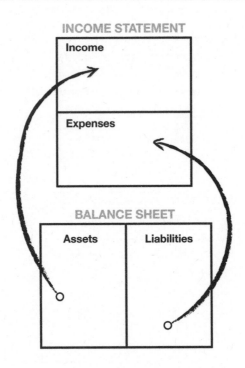

The Power of Words

Here are two important definitions, distinctions that rich dad made in helping us understand the difference between an asset and a liability.

Assets put money in your pocket whether you work or not.

Liabilities take money from your pocket even if they go up in value.

Q: *So the direction of cash flowing determines if something is an asset or liability?*

A: Yes.

Q: *So a house could be an asset if the house was putting money in your pocket?*

A: You got it. Anything can be an asset or liability, as defined by the direction of cash flow. Most people have money slipping through their fingers because they insist their house or car is an asset.

Tax Lessons from Tom

Liabilities and Cash Flow

Another way to describe a financial statement is a "statement of financial condition." A person's financial condition is good if their cash inflows exceed their cash outflows. If you had no job to rely on, your cash inflows would be determined solely by your assets and your cash outflows would be determined solely by your liabilities. So *assets* can very literally be defined as something that creates cash inflows and *liabilities* can be defined as something that creates cash outflows. The difference between your assets and liabilities, or cash inflows and outflows, is called your net worth, or wealth.

To review, the six words at the heart of financial literacy are *income, expense, asset, liability,* and *cash flow.*

Q: *Is that why you named your game CASHFLOW, combining the two words into one?*

A: Yes. Because in the real world of money, the ability to control the direction of cash flow is most important. The rich know how to control cash flowing in and the poor and middle class cannot control cash flowing out.

Q: *Is that why the world is in financial crisis? Because our leaders are creating liabilities and cash is flowing out?*

A: Yes. And on top of that our leaders are printing money to cover the cash flowing out.

A Change of Focus

The millionaires next door focus on these two assets.

INCOME STATEMENT

Income
Expenses

BALANCE SHEET

Assets	Liabilities
Savings Stocks	

The biggest problem today is these two assets—savings and stocks—are toxic.

Remember that from 1971 to 2000, people who saved money and invested for the long term in the stock market were doing fine. Then, in 2000, the world changed.

A financially literate person is able to look at the chart below—a chart we've previously reviewed—and understand what the chart is telling us.

The Giant Crash of 1929

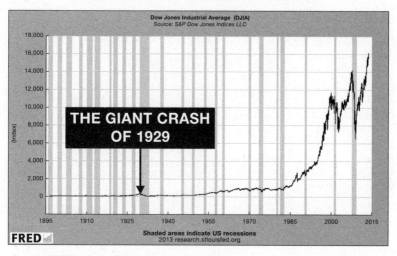

Source: FRED–Federal Reserve Economic Data

Q: *Why are you scaring me?*

A: That isn't my intention. And I know it may be frightening, but my reason for the work I do in support of financial education is to prepare people for what is coming next.

Q: *What will happen next?*

A: I don't really know. No one really knows. We have never been here before.

On September 7, 2010, Warren Buffett said:

> *"The one thing I will tell you is the worst investment you can have is cash. Everybody is talking about cash being king and all that sort of thing. Cash is going to become worth less over time."*

People who followed Buffett's advice—those who got out of cash positions and into the stock market in 2010—did very well. The problem is, as I am writing this book in 2017, the stock market is at all-time highs. The question is: Can Warren save them in this crash?

Look again at Buffett's performance during the first three crashes of this century.

Berkshire Hathaway vs. S&P 500 (5-Year Return)

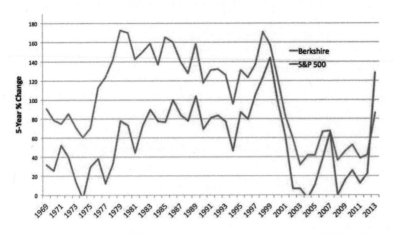

Source: Business Insider/Andy Kiersz, data from Berkshire Hathaway and Yahoo! Finance

The chart shows the markets climbing again. The question is: Can investors—even those as savvy as Warren Buffett—not lose money in the coming crash?

Are You Financially Illiterate?

As you consider these actions and reactions, these lessons on financial literacy and illiteracy, think about how you've responded. What have you been thinking and feeling? Below I have summarized how financially illiterate people are likely to respond in the real world—if there is another crash:

Financial illiteracy immobilizes people.

Financial illiteracy destroys self-esteem.

Financial illiteracy causes a person to be frustrated and upset.

Financially illiterate people create fixed ideas.

Financially illiterate people believe they are victims.

Financial illiteracy causes blindness.

Financial illiteracy causes poverty.

Financially illiterate people make poor investors.

Financial illiteracy causes poor judgment.

Financial illiteracy causes a person to hate life.

Financial illiteracy can lead to unethical actions.

Q: *So what can a financially illiterate person do?*

A: Start getting financially literate. Start by understanding the six basic words of financial literacy:

1. Income
2. Expense
3. Asset
4. Liability
5. Cash
6. Flow

Challenge yourself to:

Understand how cash flow determines if something is an asset or a liability.

Understand why a house is not an asset.

Understand why savers are losers.

Understand why your investment portfolio may be a liability, not an asset.

Understand why the markets are in turmoil.

Understand why the two primary assets of the millionaires next door, savings and stocks, may become liabilities.

Understand why, "It's the money, stupid."

If you can understand and explain these principles and ideas, you are on your way to becoming a financial genius.

Part Two

SUMMARY

Money is a language. Learning to be rich is much like learning a foreign language. It takes time, practice, and dedication.

Poor people speak the same language. They speak the language of poverty. They think in the words of the poor and use those words when they communicate. Their most frequently used words are, *"I can't afford it"* and *"I can't do it."* Until those words change, little else will change.

As Henry Ford said:

> *"If you think you can you can.*
> *If you think you can't you can't.*
> *Either way you are right."*

The middle class speaks the same language. The favorite words of the middle class are: *job security, steady paycheck,* and *benefits.* They avoid the words *risk* and *debt.* They think the idea of *saving money* is smart. And it was, until 1971. Until a person's words change, little else will change.

The language of the rich is different. The rich, those with financial education, speak different languages. Entrepreneurs speak a different language than employees. Real estate investors speak a different language than stock market investors. A real estate investor will use words like *cap rate* and a stock market investor will talk about

P/E ratio, both meaning almost the same thing. The point is, *"Words become flesh."*

Got Real Financial Education?

Part Two has been about:

> *What financial education is not.*
> *What is financial illiteracy?*

Part Three will focus on

What is real financial education?

The good news is that real financial education begins with words, the real language of money—the language of the rich. And the best news of all: Words *do* become flesh and words are free.

Part Three

WHAT IS REAL FINANCIAL EDUCATION?

Introduction to Part Three

DEBT AND TAXES

I bet a lot of people would agree with me if I said that the two nastiest words in the world's financial vocabulary are *debt* and *taxes*.

Debt and taxes are the real reason for the growing gap between the rich and everyone else.

That is why 1913 is a critical year in world history. In 1913, the U.S. Federal Reserve Bank was created. It was also the year the 16th amendment was ratified, the action that led to the creation of the Internal Revenue Service—the dreaded, and often feared U.S. tax department.

These two institutions needed to co-exist before what Dr. Fuller called GRUNCH, the Gross Universal Cash Heist, could take place.

Today, debt and taxes are like a cancer, eating away at the heart and soul of the poor and middle class. The U.S. national debt is a disaster waiting to happen. Yet, on the other side of the coin, debt and taxes continue to make the rich richer.

Real financial education is not about which stocks, bonds, ETFs, or mutual funds to buy. Real financial education is not about diversification. As Warren Buffett states:

> **"Diversification** *is protection against ignorance. It makes little sense if you know what you are doing."*

How can a person know what they are doing if they know so little about debt and taxes?

Whenever I say, "I make millions and pay very little taxes—legally," most people's hearts go into cardiac arrest and their minds slam shut. I doubt there are many people more feared than the taxman. Few things are more painful than a government tax audit. Yet it does not have to be that way, if—as Buffett states—"you know what you are doing."

Having Tom Wheelwright as my mentor, teacher, and tax advisor gives me tremendous confidence to do what I do daily as an entrepreneur and professional investor. Before I do anything that could cross the line, I check in with Tom. Life is so much easier if you follow the rules, especially the tax rules and laws.

As Tom always says, "The tax rules are primarily incentives, government guidelines on how to be a partner with the government, doing what the government wants and needs done." That is why tax laws throughout the world favor entrepreneurs and big businesses.

Simply put:

The tax code punishes those in the E and S quadrants.

The tax code rewards those in the B and I quadrants.

This is why *real financial education* must start with debt and taxes. *Real financial education* must look at the other side of the coin of debt and taxes.

Real financial education must teach the student how debt and taxes make the rich richer. *Real Financial education* must also teach the student how debt and taxes can make them richer too.

And this is why I asked my personal tax advisor, Tom Wheelwright, to be my adjuvant for this book. Debt and taxes are the heartbeat of *real financial education*.

Tax Lessons from Tom

The Real Purpose of the Tax Law

While tax laws do raise revenue for the government, they also serve a very important purpose in encouraging people to follow government policy. Governments around the world want businesses to hire more people and investors to create more housing, energy, and food. That's why there are so many tax incentives in the B and the I quadrants.

Chapter Nine

WHY THE RICH
PLAY MONOPOLY

Poor Dad:
"Get a job."

Rich Dad:
"Don't work for money."

Over the years I have attended many seminars, conferences, and lectures on money. The speakers have had one thing in common: They made things complex, confusing, and frustrating.

Many of them seemed to speak a foreign language. I suspected many used "financial jargon"—not to communicate effectively, but to feel superior. They wanted to prove they were smarter than we were.

Real financial education does not have to be complex or confusing. I think of the words often attributed to Albert Einstein: *"If you can't explain it to a six year old, you don't understand it yourself."*

Real financial education can be very simple, as simple as playing *Monopoly*.

Three Incomes

When you advise a young person, "Go to school, get a job, work hard, save money, and invest for the long term in a 401(k)," what is missing is a little financial education on *taxes*.

The person who advises a young person to follow the *"Go to school and get a job..."* formula for success should also add, *"And you will pay the highest percentages in taxes."*

If the young person knew that tiny bit of information, they might ask, *"How do I pay lower percentages in taxes?"* That question would lead a person to ask other questions like, "What is real financial education?"

That question, and ones like it, would lead a person to stand on the *edge* of the coin—a vantage point from which they could see both sides. He or she could look at the side of the coin where the rich live, the side of the coin that *does not work for money.*

Real financial education on taxes does not have to be complex. The subject of money begins with income, the type of income a person works for. There are three types of income.

1. Ordinary income
2. Portfolio income
3. Passive income

Ordinary income is the highest taxed of the three incomes.

When you advise or encourage a person to "get a job," that person starts thinking like an employee and working for *ordinary income.*

When a person says, "Go back to school and take your career to the next level," that too means, eventually, working for *ordinary income.*

When a person advises someone to "save money," that, too, makes a statement on taxes. The interest from savings is taxes as *ordinary income.*

When someone advises "save for retirement in a 401(k)," the long-term ramifications of this is that the income from a 401(k) is *ordinary income.*

Tax Lessons from Tom

Ordinary Income Is the Worst Income

Portfolio income and passive income are taxed at special rates and have special tax benefits. The government prefers portfolio and passive income, so it provides an incentive to earn income that is portfolio or passive. All other income is ordinary. The government chooses not to give a tax incentive for people to work or save money.

The tax incentive for setting money aside for retirement, such as in a 401(k) in the United States or RRSP in Canada, is the ability to defer the tax on the income until it is pulled out. In addition to taxing the (401)k at ordinary tax rates, the tax law penalizes someone who pulls it out before retirement age. So not only is it taxed at the highest rate, you have to leave it in until you retire or pay both a high tax rate and a penalty.

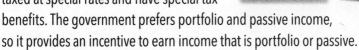

Q: *So going to school, getting a job, saving money, and investing for the long term in certain government-sponsored retirement plans is working for ordinary income?*

A: Yes.

Q: *And when a person becomes an entrepreneur and moves from employee in the E quadrant to entrepreneur in the S quadrant, the entrepreneurs in the S quadrant pay an even higher percentage of income in taxes?*

A: Yes.

Q: *Why is that?*

A: The simple and short answer is because they work for money. Remember, rich dad's lesson #1 from *Rich Dad Poor Dad* is, "The rich don't work for money." Also remember that, after 1971, all money became debt. Why work for money when more and more money is being printed? Why get out of debt when money is debt? Keep in mind that it all comes down to one thing: It's the money, stupid.

Schools teach students to work for money. That is the primary reason why the gap between the rich and the poor and middle class grows.

Giving people more money will not help. More entitlement programs only make the poor and middle class poorer, because entitlement programs are paid for with taxes, taxes paid by the poor and middle class, the people that work for money.

Q: *Is that fair?*

A: There's that f-word again. Who said anything about *fair?* I didn't say it was fair. If life was fair I would look like Brad Pitt. What is *not* fair is the lack of *real* financial education in schools. Without real financial education, billions of people are in financial crisis.

Schools teach students to work for *ordinary income.* Period. That is where the problem begins.

Income of the Rich

The rich work for *portfolio income* and *passive income.*

Portfolio Income is also called *capital gains.* A capital gain occurs when you buy low and sell high. For example, you buy a share of stock for $10 and you sell for $16. You have a capital gain of $6 per share. The $6 is *portfolio income.* The same is true when you buy real estate in a crash and then wait until it increases in value before selling it. Buying and selling real estate for a gain is the same thing: you buy low and sell high.

Technically, *ordinary income* occurs when you work for money. And, technically, *portfolio income* occurs any time you buy low and sell high… when your money works for you, instead of you working hard for money.

Portfolio income is taxed at 20% in the United States.

Tax Lessons from Tom

Portfolio Income around the World

It's not just the United States that favors investment. Most countries have a lower tax rate for portfolio income than for ordinary income. Most governments want their citizens to invest, so they give them an incentive to invest–special tax rates for portfolio income.

Passive Income is *cash flowing from an asset.* Your asset is producing money. In real estate, passive income is called *rental income.* For example, if I buy a rental property for $100,000 and my net monthly rental income is $1,000 a month, the $1,000 is *passive income*

Passive income from real estate is the lowest-taxed income, sometimes at 0%.

As you can tell, this is where things can begin to get confusing. There are many different words saying basically the same things. Real estate guys say it one way, stock guys say the same thing differently, and bond guys speak another foreign language.

So to keep things simple, I just remember there are three types of income: *ordinary, portfolio,* and *passive.* If I am at a conference and the speaker is speaking a "foreign" language, I simply raise my hand and ask, *"Is that ordinary income, portfolio income, or passive income?"* If the speaker does not know the differences between the three types of income, that person does not know what they are talking about. As I've quoted earlier in this chapter: *"If you can't explain it to a six year old, you don't understand it yourself."*

Q: *So real financial education must include knowing the differences between the three types of income?*

A: Yes. That is where the gap between rich, poor, and middle class begins. It begins with what type of income they work for.

Playing Monopoly

Rich dad used the game of *Monopoly* as a teaching tool. The board game was his classroom. He was teaching us to not work for money, for *ordinary income*. He was teaching us to work for *portfolio* and *passive income*. For example, if I had one green house and the rental income from that house was $10, that $10 was *passive income*, the lowest taxed of the three incomes.

Q: *So at a young age, you knew the difference between the three different types of income?*

A: I did. As the Introduction to Part Three of this book states, real financial education must teach the student about debt and taxes. Most importantly, *how debt and taxes can make them richer.* Playing *Monopoly* laid the foundation for understanding how debt and taxes could make me richer, by understanding the three types of income.

After playing *Monopoly,* rich dad would take us to see his real "green houses," his rental properties. He used words like *rental income* and *cash flow.* He would always tell us, "Someday these green houses will be a red hotel."

After looking at rich dad's green houses, I would go home and my poor dad would ask, "Have you done your homework? If you don't get good grades, you won't go to a good school and you won't get a good job."

Q: *So one dad was advising you to work for ordinary income and the other for portfolio and passive income?*

A: Yes. Obviously, being a 9-year-old kid, I did not yet understand the three types of income—or debt and taxes. But rich dad was laying the foundation for my future. I was on the other side of the coin… and I could see my future. I could see that my journey to the other side of the coin would be by learning to play *Monopoly* in real life.

Big Red Hotels

Ten years later, when I was 19, I returned home to Hawaii from school in New York for the grand opening of rich dad's red hotel, right smack in the middle of Waikiki Beach. It was on one of most prestigious pieces of real estate in Hawaii and the world.

Today my wife Kim and I own a big red hotel in Arizona, with hundreds of employees, on a property that includes five golf courses. All we did was play *Monopoly in* real life.

Kim and I did not get rich working for *ordinary income*. We worked for *portfolio* and *passive income*.

Q: *Is that why you and your wife developed your game CASHFLOW? To teach people how to understanding investing?*

A: Yes. Kim and I were financially free by 1996. Kim was 37 and I was 47. It took 10 years. As a young married couple, we had started with nothing. We achieved financial freedom without jobs, without saving money, and without a 401(k).

When people asked us how we achieved financial freedom, we could not explain exactly how we did it. We even tried playing *Monopoly* with people, in an attempt to explain the process we used. That led us to develop the *CASHFLOW* game, launching the commercial version in 1996.

Rich Dad Poor Dad was self-published in 1997, more as a brochure to explain the *CASHFLOW* game than as a "book." It was a "brochure" I wrote to sell the game. As you know by now, every publisher we approached turned the book down.

Q: *The publishers you contacted could not see the other side of the coin?*

A: That's what we assumed. They seemed to have difficulty understanding why *the rich do not work for money,* why *savers are losers,* and why *your house is not an asset.* Most of the publishers were employees who worked for money, *ordinary income.* My book and the *CASHFLOW* game teach people about *portfolio* income and, especially, *passive income.*

Q: *The publishers may not have understood the message in your book, but Oprah Winfrey must have. Is that why she invited you on her show in 2000?*

A: Oprah is one of the richest women in the world. She understood the story of rich dad and poor dad. Her life started on the poor side of the coin and moved to the rich side. Today, she definitely lives on the other side of the coin. Oprah does not need a job.

Why the Stock Market Bubble?

Earlier in this book I cited *financialization* as one reason why the rich get richer. The financialization industry brought us this financial crisis by building weapons of mass financial destruction, a mysterious product known as *derivatives.* The financialization industry keeps the world economy in a bubble, pumping in trillions in debt and keeping interest rates below zero, in the hope that the final crash does not arrive.

Financialization affects corporate executives' pay. According to the Economic Policy Institute, CEO pay has grown exponentially since 1970. Since 1970, CEO pay has risen almost 1,000%. Employees' pay has risen roughly 11% during that same period of time.

Corporate Executives Do Not Work for Money

In the corporate world, a large part of an executive's compensation is in *stock options*, rather than a paycheck. The top executives do not want large paychecks. They do not want ordinary income.

Let's say the CEO has an option to buy his company's stock at $10 a share. The CEO does a great job and the stock price goes up to $16. The CEO then *exercises the optio*n to buy the stock at $10 a share—and often sells the shares immediately for $16, netting $6 per share of profit. If he or she has one million shares, the capital gains are $6 million. Capital gains taxes on $6 million in portfolio income is a lot less than ordinary income taxes on $6 million in salary. If the CEO had received $6 million as *ordinary income*, a paycheck, he or she would have paid approximately 45% in federal and state taxes.

$6 million at 45% = $2.7 million in taxes

Choosing to take $6 million as long-term capital gains, or *portfolio income*, he or she would have paid approximately 25% in federal and state taxes.

$6 million at 25% = $1.5 million in taxes.

Employees of the same company work for *ordinary income* while the executives work for *portfolio income.* Yet another reason why the rich are getting richer.

If an executive is confident that he or she can get the employees to work hard and increase the stock price of the company, the executive may take $1 in salary, *ordinary income*, and the rest in stock options, or *portfolio income.* Lee Iacocca did this as CEO of Chrysler and so did Steve Jobs at Apple. Again, the rich do not work for money. And one reason is taxes.

Bubble Vision

After the 2008 crash, U.S. businesses were struggling to grow. If the business did not grow and share prices did not go up, CEOs and executives would not make a lot of money.

This is when massive financialization took off. With interest rates at all-time lows, CEOs began borrowing money, using the company's good credit with banks to buy the company's stock. It was called *share buy back*. What share buy back means is that the CEO and his or her staff cannot grow the business. So rather than borrow money to invest in R&D, research and development, and creating new products and markets—which would make the company stronger—the CEO borrows money and invests in the stock market, buying back the company shares and pushing the share price of the company up. The CEO then sells his shares, earning *portfolio income* instead of *ordinary income*.

Most mom-and-pops, the millionaire-next-door investors, think *share buy backs* are wonderful. Their retirement portfolio goes up as the share prices go up. They believe the company is stronger. They believe the CEO has done a great job growing the business.

The problem is that in most cases the company is left weakened, uncompetitive without new products or vision for the future, and deeply in debt. The executives then exit the company floating on "golden parachutes" with bags filled with *portfolio income.*

The employees are left on a sinking, debt-laden ship, still working for *ordinary income*, saving money to earn interest (which is also *ordinary income*), and investing in a 401(k) retirement plan… also for *ordinary income.*

Without real financial education, how would an employee know why working, saving, and investing for ordinary income is not the best idea? How would an employee know why the gap between the rich and themselves keeps growing?

Time to Strike

After a while, the workers know something is wrong. They smell a rat. Their wages are not rising. Union leaders call for a strike, demanding higher wages. The workers win, they earn more *ordinary income.*

Higher wages make the company weaker. The company becomes a "take over target." The existing board of directors, the same people who made millions in *portfolio income*, agrees it is time for a change. They have made enough money. So they sell to a new owner. Once the company is sold, the new owners "clean house." Very often one of the first things they do is fire employees.

Laid off workers go back to school, many taking on student loans, the worst type of debt known to man, hoping to find a new job… working, again, for *ordinary income*. And the gap between rich and everyone grows wider.

Rather than going to union meetings, demanding more *ordinary income*, or going back to school for more *ordinary income*, the employees should have played *Monopoly* at lunchtime. They could have learned why the rent from a green house was better than a paycheck.

Tax Lessons from Tom

Education Taxes

When someone goes back to school to get a job, the cost of the education is not deductible. This is because they are getting an entire new profession. If they go to seminars for financial education to improve their investing, however, the education can be deductible as an improvement in their business and investing skills.

Chapter Ten

PHANTOM INCOME:
INCOME OF THE RICH

Poor Dad:
"I need my paycheck."

Rich Dad:
"I don't need a paycheck."

Describing phantom income is like attempting to describe a ghost in a room. This is a very important chapter and I have done my best to keep it simple. Phantom income is the income of the very rich. It is income that very few people are aware of.

Here is my suggestion: If you find this chapter confusing, partner with a friend, someone who likes math, read this chapter on your own, and then discuss the chapter together. If the concept of phantom income is still not clear, talk to an accountant and do your best to understand this very important subject. Without real financial education most people are blind to phantom income. This chapter is very important because phantom income is the income of the rich.

A Higher Level of Financial Intelligence

When I returned from Vietnam in 1973, rich dad suggested I begin my financial education by taking classes on real estate investing.

"Get my real estate license?" I asked.

Rich dad laughed and said, "No. Real estate licenses are for people in the S quadrant. You want financial education for the I quadrant."

Real estate agents work for *ordinary income* and real estate investors work for *portfolio* and *passive income.* There is nothing wrong with having a real estate license, but most real estate brokers are not real estate investors. As rich dad often said, "The reason they are called *brokers* is because they are *broker than you."*

At the time, I was still flying for the Marine Corps. One night, after a night mission, I returned home to my condo in Waikiki. It was late and I turned on the TV, and caught an infomercial on real estate investing. The promoter promised to teach me how to buy real estate for "no money down." Since Marine Corps pilots did not make much money, the idea of buying real estate, in Hawaii—some of the most expensive real estate in the world—for *no money down* interested me. I called the number on the TV screen and made a reservation for the initial "free seminar."

At the free seminar I saw many people just like me, people looking for a different path in life, people who were tired of their 9-to-5 jobs. The seminar that was being promoted was three days long and cost $385—a fortune at the time, and nearly half of my salary as a Marine Corps pilot.

When I asked rich dad if he thought my going to a seminar a good thing or a bad thing, he smiled and said, "How would I know? I have not done the course. There is only one way to find out. You just do it. You will always learn something. Doing something is better than what most people do… which is nothing."

Academic Man vs. Seminar Man

This was another difference between rich dad and poor dad. Poor dad was an academic man. He believed in traditional education. If a Brand-Name University did not present the course, it was not real education. If the instructor did not have PhD after their name, the instructor was not a real teacher.

Rich dad was a seminar man. He especially loved Dale Carnegie courses. To him, they were practical, useful, and a relatively inexpensive investment in terms of both money and time. Rich dad was not concerned with the teacher's credentials. He was more concerned about the teacher's charisma. If the instructor was boring, he was certain the Carnegie company wouldn't tolerate it. They'd fire the instructor. So he was pretty sure that the instructors would hold his attention and teach him a few things.

Poor dad was especially concerned about degrees and titles. He loved moving from high school valedictorian, to Bachelor of Arts degree, to Master's degree, to PhD. Titles and degrees are important in the world of the E and S quadrants.

Rich dad was only concerned about achieving success in the B and I quadrants.

Warren Buffett: Seminar Man

Even Warren Buffett attends seminars. I heard that he once said, "I do not display my college degree on my office wall. I do proudly display my certificate from my Dale Carnegie public speaking course. I had to learn how to keep my hands and feet from shaking, whenever I spoke at shareholders' meetings."

Warren hosts one of the most popular seminars in the world, the Berkshire Hathaway annual investor conference. It is called: Woodstock for Capitalists.

Real Teacher

The three-day real estate seminar was fantastic. My instructor was a *real,* real estate investor. He was rich, he was financially free, and he was happy. Everything I wanted to be.

The course was practical, no B.S. The instructor used real-life examples, not textbook theory. He spoke of his wins and his losses. And, like rich dad, he emphasized the importance of mistakes—that mistakes were priceless taps on the shoulder, telling you, "Wake up, you don't know everything… here's something you need to learn."

He spoke of the importance of having good partners and the painful lessons from bad partners, especially dishonest ones. He spoke of the value of trust, honor, and humility, of treating everyone you worked with kindness and respect. To him, thinking you were smarter or better than the next person was a sin, a crime against your fellow human.

At the end of the three days, I discovered that being a real estate investor was not about making money. Being a real estate investor was about being an entrepreneur in residential real estate, providing safe, affordable housing for people. If you did a good job, you made a lot of money.

If you did a good job, *the banks would lend you more money.* And, if you did a good job, *the government gave you tax breaks.* You were a partner with the government, doing what the government wanted done.

Being a real, real estate investor was not about "flipping" property for *capital gains.* People who flip houses are *property traders*, a different class of *property investor.* People who flip property tend to make housing more expensive; they want prices to go up so flippers pay a higher tax rate.

Tax Lessons from Tom

Flipping Creates Ordinary Income

Flipping requires the personal efforts of the investor. So flipping is taxed as ordinary income and flippers pay the same tax rates as anybody else in the S quadrant.

Most stock-market investors are like real estate flippers. They do not really want the asset; they just want the price of the asset to go up. As soon as there is enough of a capital gain, they sell—often selling in a matter of days or even hours. That is how they make money. That is why taxes on *capital gains, especially gains from flipping stocks,* are higher than taxes for passive investors, especially real estate investors who invest for *cash flow.*

Traders believe in the "Greater Fool Theory" of investing. A trader buys, then waits for a fool greater than they are—someone willing to pay a higher price than they paid. Traditionally, a trader does not add any value to the asset. A few real estate flippers do "fix-up" the property then flip it. Flipping a property or a stock is working for income. Stock and property flippers pay a higher tax rate than real, real estate investors.

Market Crashes

Flippers or traders do well as long as the Greater Fool shows up. When fools stop buying, markets start crashing. That is what happened in 2000, 2007, and 2008. Crashes occur when fools stop being foolish.

Cash flow investors wait for market crashes. Fools run and hide and the real investor comes out of hibernation, looking for bargains.

Phantom Cash Flow

The instructor at the three-day seminar went far beyond how to find and buy property for nothing down. Like rich dad, he spoke about phantom cash flow, the invisible income. He taught, "Phantom cash flow is the *real* income of the rich. Phantom income is the income the poor and middle class cannot see."

In other words, he was saying *phantom cash flow* is **not** *ordinary, portfolio,* or *passive income*—income you can see. Phantom cash flow is invisible to people without financial education. *Phantom cash flow is invisible income, a derivative of debt and taxes.*

Q: *Debt and taxes produce phantom cash flow?*

A: Yes. That is why real financial education is centered around debt and taxes. Always remember this: Real financial education is about debt, taxes, and phantom cash flow… the invisible income of the rich.

The remainder of this chapter is about how you can see the invisible, the ghosts in the room. Phantom income.

Please note: All the examples I offer are extremely simple—for instructional purposes only. For those who want greater detail, I will list seven books that I believe are essential for those who want to live their lives in the I quadrant.

Debt Is Phantom Cash Flow

When people put money down, a deposit, on a house, they generally use after-tax dollars. For example, let's say a $100,000 property requires a 20% down payment. That means the property buyer must come up with $20,000. If the investor is in the 40% income tax bracket, that $20,000 really cost the investor approximately $35,000 in *ordinary income*, or *paycheck* money. Approximately $15,000 went to the government in taxes.

Borrow the Money

The question is: What if the investor borrowed the $20,000, rather than used his or her own, after-tax paycheck money?

The answer is the investor saved $15,000. The $15,000 is *phantom income*, money the investor did not have to work for, did not pay taxes on, and did not have to save.

Q: *So by using debt, the investor is ahead of the game by $15,000? Isn't that like giving a runner a head start in the race?*

A: It is. While mom and pop are saving *after tax* dollars for a down payment, *the professional investor who knows how to use debt as money* is way down the road. The professional investor is on to the next investment before mom and pop leave the house.

Q: *Just because the professional investor uses debt and the amateur uses after-tax savings.*

A: You're getting it. Think about it. Think about how much time and money you would save if you did not have to work, pay taxes, and live frugally just to save the $20,000 down payment?

Q: *You mean just borrow the $20,000?*

A: Yes. Think about this: $20,000 is *not* a lot of money for many people. Yet what happens when you need $200,000, or $2 million—or $20 million—for a down payment?

Q: *I could not afford the down payment. So the rich get richer because they know how to borrow the money for larger down payments on properties?*

A: Yes. If you are a working person in the E quadrant and you are trying work and save your way to riches, it is difficult to play the game in the I quadrant. The I quadrant is about debt, taxes, and phantom income. Without real financial education, people in the E quadrant cannot see what is *really* happening in the I quadrant.

That is why stocks, bonds, and mutual funds are best for those in the E and S quadrants. You do not need down payments for paper assets. Most people just pay cash.

Q: *So debt is the key in the I quadrant?*

A: Yes—and taxes and phantom income. Remember that debt is tax-free. You save a lot of time and money, *renting money* rather than *working* for it.

Q: *But that takes a lot of skill doesn't it?*

A: It does. And that's where financial education comes in. I'll repeat Donald Trump's words: "You know I am the king of debt" and "I love debt, but debt is tricky and it is dangerous."

Q: *So that is why rich dad suggested you take a real estate course, before becoming a real estate investor… because real estate is about debt, taxes, and phantom income?*

A: Yes.

Q: *Why didn't he teach you himself?*

A: He said he had taken me as far as he could. It was time for me to seek better teachers. That is what he did. He was constantly flying to seminars in different cities, seeking new teachers.

Rich dad often reminded me of the three wise men following a star in the heavens. Although they were already rich and wise, they never stopped seeking new and wiser teachers.

Sophisticated Investor

As stated earlier—and as a review—there are six basic words of financial education.

These are the words of a financial statement:
> income
> expense
> asset
> liability
> cash
> flow

Remember that your banker does not ask you for your report card. Your banker wants to see your financial statement. And, sadly, most people do not have one.

Next, let's review the three types of income: ordinary, portfolio, and passive.

The percentages, below, are approximate and for emphasis and illustration purposes only:

Ordinary   40%
Portfolio   20%
Passive   0%

The poor and middle class, in most cases, have only *ordinary income,* the highest taxed of the three incomes. Savings and 401(k) income are also taxed as ordinary income. The millionaire next door works for *ordinary* and *portfolio income.*

The sophisticated investor works for *phantom income.* Phantom income requires a much higher level of real financial education and literacy, because phantom income is invisible income.

The following are examples of phantom income:

Debt is tax-free money.

The phantom income from debt is the *time* and *money* you save *renting money* rather than working to earn it, paying taxes on it, and saving it.

The example used earlier explained how a $20,000 down payment really costs $35,000 in ordinary income. The $15,000 difference is phantom income—money and time saved.

You can get richer faster if you know how to use debt as money.

Appreciation is phantom income.

Appreciation occurs when the price of a property goes up. For example, a $100,000 property increases in value to $150,000. The $50,000 is phantom income known as *appreciation.*

The problem is that most people have to sell the property to get their hands on the $50,000. Selling triggers a taxable event, capital gains taxes.

If the capital gain is $50,000:

$50,000 X 20% tax = $10,000 in taxes.

A Less Expensive Way

Rather than sell a property, Kim, Ken McElroy and I have a different strategy. We pull out our $50,000 in appreciation through debt, rather than sell the property. Homeowners do this all the time—it's called a *home equity loan.*

The *appreciation*, the phantom income, comes out as debt and into our pockets tax-free.

The Big Difference

The *big* difference is that the *tenants pay* the interest expense on the $50,000 on our rental property. In the case of a home equity loan, the *homeowners themselves pay* the interest on the loan.

More often than not, many homeowners take the $50,000 loan and pay off credit card debt and other higher-interest loans, like school loans. This may reduce a family's total monthly interest expense, but they are not getting ahead financially.

The professional investor will take the $50,000 and use it as a down payment on more rental properties. Let's say the professional investor takes the $50,000 from an existing property and acquires two more rental properties. Their financial statement now has three rental properties in the Asset column, instead of just one.

Q: *But didn't the investor's debt go up—with two new mortgages?*

A: Yes, but if the investor was a good investor, so did his passive income. That pays the interest on the new mortgages, and puts *passive income* into his or her pocket.

Q: *And the investor receives more phantom income?*

A: The following are more examples of an investor's phantom income.

Tax Lessons from Tom

More Real Estate = More Phantom Income

Suppose your one rental property cost $100,000. You have no debt and you have $100,000 of property, all of which came from after-tax income. Instead, you borrow $200,000 and buy three properties. Now you have real estate worth $300,000. Let's say your appreciation is 10% on your properties. If you have one property, your appreciation, or phantom income is $10,000 ($100,000 x 10%). However, if you have three properties worth $300,000, your appreciation or phantom income is $30,000 ($300,000 x 10%). In this case, your debt tripled your phantom income.

Here are more examples of an investor's phantom income:

Amortization is phantom income.

Amortization is the reduction of your debt. Every time you make a mortgage, car, or credit card payment your loan balance is being amortized, or paid off.

Mom and pop *amortize* their debt with after-tax, ordinary income dollars. They use their money. That's very different than real estate investors' debt, debt that a *tenant amortizes*. The reduction in debt is another source of phantom income for professional investors.

I love real estate because my tenants amortize my debt, not me. Remember **good** *debt is your debt that someone else pays for.* Every month, Kim and I get richer because every month our tenants are *amortizing* our debt.

Depreciation is phantom income.

Depreciation is also known as *wear and tear*. The tax department gives you tax write-offs because, in theory, your investment property is going down in value due to wear and tear.

Even if your property is *appreciating*, going up in value, the taxman gives you a tax break for *depreciation, as if the* property's going down in value.

Depreciation is a major source of phantom income for professional real estate investors.

Tax Lessons from Tom

The Magic of Depreciation

In Chapter 7 of my book, *Tax-Free Wealth*, I explain in great detail the magic of depreciation. It truly is phantom income. Imagine receiving a tax deduction that you don't have to pay for. Even if you borrow the money to buy the real estate, you get a deduction for depreciation. Even if the property goes up in value, you get a deduction for depreciation. Most countries allow this deduction, but only for property that produces cash flow. Personal residences do not create a depreciation deduction.

Why Savers Are Losers

Savers are losers because:

1. Savers *pay taxes on interest earnings*—often with after-tax dollars from *ordinary income.*

2. Savers are losing money as *the purchasing power of their savings* goes down due to *the banking system.* (Both Quantitative Easing, QE, and fractional reserve banking are factors.)

    Q: *So savers are taxed while their money loses value?*
    A: Yes.

    Q: *And real estate investors win because they are given tax breaks as their property appreciates in value?*
    A: Yes.

This next example is how phantom income really makes the rich richer.

McDonald's Money is phantom cash flow.

Ray Kroc once said, McDonald's is a real estate company. McDonald's is one of the world's largest chains of fast-food restaurants *and* a real estate company for a reason: phantom income.

Let the CASHFLOW Quadrant tell the story.

McDonald's hamburger business

McDonald's real estate business

Let's say McDonald's fast-food business earns $1 million in *taxable income*. And let's say McDonald's real estate business has $1 million in *depreciation*.

The $1 million in *taxable income* from the business is offset by $1 million in *depreciation* from the real estate business. That means McDonald's fast-food business *pays zero in taxes.*

Tax Lessons from Tom

Taxable Income

If McDonald's did not have any real estate, it would pay about $450,000 in taxes on its $1 million of taxable income ($1,000,000 X 45% tax rate). The depreciation deduction reduces McDonald's taxable income to zero ($1,000,000 income less $1,000,000 deduction). So McDonald's pays *no tax* on its $1 million of fast-food income and saves $450,000 in taxes.

Q: *So McDonald's gets richer many ways, other than just income?*

A: Yes. A few more examples are:

1. The $1 million in *depreciation from real estate is phantom income.*

2. Their real estate *appreciation is phantom income.*

3. The increase in the value of McDonald's hamburger business is phantom income.

4. The debt on both the business and real estate is being *amortized* by the business, which is *more phantom income.*

5. Many U.S. companies earn income outside the United States and keep that income outside the country, out of reach of U.S. taxes. More phantom income.

6. This list could go on and on, depending on how smart the business tax strategies are, on how smart their tax strategists, their "Tom Wheelwrights," are.

Employees at McDonald's

Meanwhile the *employees* at McDonald's work for a paycheck, save money, struggle to get out of debt, and invest in a 401(k)—all subject to *ordinary income taxes.*

And we wonder why the rich get richer.

Q: *Do you follow the McDonald's formula in your business?*

A: We do. All you have to do is change "McDonald's" to "The Rich Dad Company" in the B-quadrant.

Let the CASHFLOW Quadrant tell the story.

McDonald's hamburger business

McDonald's real estate business

The Rich Dad Company

Robert Kiyosaki's real estate company

One difference is that we bring all income earned overseas back to the United States, where we're headquartered. We believe that's the right thing to do.

Q: *Even if you bring all your income from The Rich Dad Company on shore, you can still pay zero taxes?*

A: Yes. When we make more money in The Rich Dad Company in the B quadrant, we buy more real estate in the I-quadrant businesses.

Q: *So you get richer in both the B and I quadrants. You also increase income, increase debt, pay less in taxes, and increase phantom income?*

A: You're getting it.

Q: *Can someone in the E and S quadrants do the same thing? Can they receive phantom income?*

A: Yes. But they must be a *professional investor in the I quadrant*. People like *the millionaire next door* do not qualify. They tend to invest in stocks, bonds, mutual funds, ETFs, and pension plans. Passive investments for passive investors do not receive the same levels of phantom income.

Q: *So is that why you talked about taking real estate seminars before investing?*

A: Yes. Investing in real estate requires far more financial education than investing in stocks, bonds, mutual funds, and ETFs.

Understanding the Asset Classes

Paper assets are liquid. If you make a mistake investing in paper assets, you can get in and get out quickly. You can cut your losses immediately.

If, on the other hand, you make a mistake in real estate, the mistake could take you down into bankruptcy. Real estate is not liquid. You cannot cut your losses quickly.

Q: *What real estate courses do you recommend?*

A: There are many companies offering real estate courses. Rich Dad does, too. The Rich Dad Company offers many real estate coaching options and courses. While I believe Rich Dad offers the best courses and coaching programs, it is important for you to decide which programs are best for you.

Another resource you can use is Rich Dad Radio—and our a weekly radio program, with podcast access anywhere in the world via RichDad.com. Every week Kim and I interview cutting-edge thinkers on a wide variety of topics that are especially relevant to entrepreneurs and professional investors. I also encourage you to check out RDTV… at RichDad.com/RDTV

Start with Books

The greatest teachers in the world are in books. And the best news is that books are inexpensive and teachers can go into greater detail. Best of all, perhaps, is that they teach on *your* schedule, when you have the time—and they come to you. If you do not understand something, the teacher is happy when you can go back and reread the parts you did not understand.

Over the years I have asked my personal advisors to write books, explaining in detail what they do. All of my Rich Dad Advisors are entrepreneurs, self-made successes, and geniuses in their different fields of work.

There are Advisor books for the S and B quadrants, and books for the I quadrant.

If you want to learn more about phantom income and the I quadrant, there are several of the Advisor books that I recommend.

Rich Dad Advisor Ken McElroy has written three books for people interested in investing in real estate from the I quadrant. Ken, Kim, and I have made millions together, often using 100% debt, much of which is tax-free. Ken is one of the brightest minds in real estate today—and an expert on using debt to acquire multi-million-dollar real estate projects. Ken McElroy's books are:

The ABCs of Real Estate Investing
The ABCs of Property Management
The Advanced Guide to Real Estate Investing

You might also enjoy Garrett Sutton's book *Loopholes of Real Estate*. He is an attorney and real estate investor.

But, of course, real estate is not for everyone. For those who prefer paper assets, Andy Tanner is my Advisor. His book is titled *Stock Market Cash Flow*. This book is priceless for the millionaire next door, a person who has a lot of money tied up in poorly-performing (or non-performing) paper assets.

Andy teaches a subject every investor needs to know: How to make money when markets are going up—and when markets are crashing. As Andy often says, "Market crashes make the rich richer."

Although paper assets do not offer the same debt, tax, and phantom income advantages that real estate does, paper assets do offer many other advantages to the professional investor in the I quadrant.

By now I'm sure you'd agree that Tom Wheelwright, my CPA and tax strategist, is a genius in how to pay less in taxes legally. He has saved Kim and me millions of dollars in taxes. Tom's Rich Dad Advisor book is titled *Tax-Free Wealth*

If you plan on becoming rich in the I quadrant, you must know how to protect your assets from two predators: lawsuits and taxes.

Garrett Sutton is an attorney, and my legal Advisor on asset protection. If not for Garrett, Kim and I would have lost everything due to frivolous lawsuits. He is a genius on asset protection and protecting your wealth from other people and the government.

To do that, you must protect your assets the way corporations in the B quadrant protect their assets. Garrett Sutton's books on asset protection are:

Start Your Own Corporation
Run Your Own Corporation
How to Use LLCs and LPs.

If you want to become a professional investor in the I quadrant, these books are essential for your library.

The Spirit of the Law

As the real estate instructor in that three-day course said many years ago, "The purpose of a residential real estate investor is to provide safe, secure, and affordable housing." If you will do that, most governments of the world will partner with you by offering tax breaks and phantom income opportunities not available to the E and S quadrants.

Tax Lessons from Tom

The Government Wants You to be Rich

The government loves partnering with investors and business owners. It partners with McDonald's by giving it $450,000 of tax breaks for investing in real estate. This is like a $450,000 investment in real estate by the government. If you build housing, the government will give you tax breaks so you don't have to take all of the risk. The government shares in the risk by giving you tax breaks against your other income.

It is essential that you follow the rules, real estate laws, finance laws, tax laws, and corporate laws. Following the spirit of the law, as well as the *letter of the law*, is required for those who live in the I quadrant.

Tax Lessons from Tom

Following the Law

By now it should be clear that the rich have different rules than the average person. They also have stricter requirements for following the rules. If someone in the E or S quadrants fudges a bit on their tax return, they get a slap on the wrist. If someone in the B or I quadrant ignores any part of the law, they go to prison. So if you want to be in the B or I quadrants, you have to learn to obey the letter and spirit of the law precisely.

Q: *Does a person need to be a big real estate investor?*

A: No. Let me give you an example of a smaller investor. Again, I will keep it as simple as possible.

Mary is a 40-year-old employee who earns $100,000 a year and pays (30% tax bracket) $30,000 a year in income tax. In her spare time, she is a professional real estate investor in the I quadrant.

After a few years, she owns 10 rental properties worth $1 million. She earns no income from her properties. The depreciation from her rental properties is $100,000 a year.

Total taxes paid on her income = $30,000

Depreciation on her rental real estate = $100,000

Taxes paid = 0 ($100,000 of income less $100,000 of depreciation)

Q: *So she earns no net rental income from her properties, yet she saves $30,000 in taxes on her ordinary income from her job, because she does not have to pay the $30,000? Her phantom income is $30,000?*

A: Yes. $30,000 is money that did not leave her checkbook.

Q: *And she is still receiving phantom income from appreciation and amortization?*

A: Correct.

Q: *And when she retires her properties will be free and clear— debt free?*

A: Yes, provided that she does not refinance or sell her properties.

Q: *And she will receive rental income for life?*

A: Yes, if she takes care of her tenants and her properties.

Q: *She won't have to worry about a giant stock market crash?*

A: No. Even if the stock market crashes and we enter another Great Depression, people still need a roof over their heads.

Q: *And she can earn more money and pay less in taxes?*

A: Yes. In *the spirit of the I quadrant*, if you take care of your tenants and your property, the government will take care of you.

A Most Important Lesson

At the end of the 3-day real estate class our instructor said, "Your education begins the moment you leave the room."

He then had us get into groups of three to five people… as we waited for his "homework" assignment.

"Your assignment is to look at 100 properties in the next 90 days. You are going to learn *how to find the best investments.* You are going to put what you've learned into action. You will make many mistakes. Your real education is about to begin," he said. "Your education begins when you knock on real estate agents' doors, go to open houses, scour the newspaper classified ads for opportunities, and drive neighborhoods looking for For Sale signs. When you find a possible deal, you are to physically inspect it, analyze it, and write up a one-page report on the pros and cons of the property, possible income growth, forecast on debt, taxes and phantom cash flow. You are to have 100 of these reports, on real properties, in the next 90 days," he instructed.

"Why are we doing this?" asked one of the students.

"Because that is what real investors do," the instructor said as he smiled at us. "This 100:1 ratio is how real investors find the best investments."

I believe there were initially five people in our group. We all agreed to do the assignment. As you might imagine, it wasn't long before some of my teammates were too busy, had kids' soccer practice, needed to work late, or had wife or husband "problems."

At the end of the 90 days there were just two of us left. We had our binders with 100 projects analyzed and evaluated. Even today, after more than four decades as a real estate investor, it was the best financial education process I have ever gone through.

I purchased my first property, a 1-bedroom /1-bath condo across the street from a beautiful beach on the Island of Maui. The property market had crashed. Buyers were in hiding. The property was in foreclosure. It was perfect for an investor. The price of the condo was $18,000—and I needed a down payment of 10%. I pulled out my credit card, charged the $1,800 down payment, purchasing the property with 100% debt. I made only $25 a month in positive cash flow—but it was an *infinite return*, because I used 100% debt, and none of my own money.

A short while later, I was offered "stupid money" for my property. The buyer offered me $42,000—more than twice what I had paid. Although I had no plan to selling, the ROI was too good to pass up. I sold the condo, placing the transaction into what is called a 1031 tax-deferred Exchange.

Q: *What is a tax-deferred exchange?*

A: It means I do not have to pay the capital gains tax on the sale. My $24,000 capital gain from the sale was tax-free, as long as I followed the rules for a 1031 Exchange.

Q: *Tax-free capital gains… more phantom income?*

A: Yes, as long as I followed the rules of the 1031, which required me to invest in more real estate. I could not spend the $24,000 on just anything. I soon purchased three more properties using the $24,000 as real-money down payments on these new properties.

Tax Lessons from Tom

1031 (Like-kind) Exchanges

In the United States, the government is willing to forego the taxes on the sale of real estate as long as it is immediately invested in other investment real estate. The gain on the sold property is transferred to the new property, so it will eventually be taxed if the investor cashes out of their real estate before they die. However, if they hold their real estate until they die, the gain is forgiven forever and no tax is ever due.

I started with debt from a credit card and kept going, following the rules of phantom money.

Q: *What is that first $18,000 property worth today?*

A: I went by it a few years ago. Properties in the same condominium complex were selling for $300,000 to $425,000. I am sure prices are higher today.

Q: *Don't you regret selling your unit?*

A: Yes and no. Due to the lessons from my three-day real course, I was able to turn my $24,000 into many millions of dollars. Today, Kim and I own over 5,000 rental properties, three hotels, five golf courses, and more—all from debt, taxes, and phantom income. So while I wish I had kept my first property, I was better off, *starting with zero and turning zero into millions.*

The Velocity of Money

Turning zero into millions of dollars is known as the *velocity of money*... how fast can I keep my money moving, acquiring more assets, then pulling the money out of those assets, without selling the assets, and buying more assets.

Another reason why the rich get richer is because the poor and middle class *park* their money in savings or invest for the long term in a pension. Rather than park their money, the I-quadrant investor keeps their money moving.

Tax Lessons from Tom

Taxes on Parking Income vs. Velocity

Income that is parked in long-term investments is taxed at capital gains rates. When an I-quadrant investor keeps their money moving through debt and investing, they pay no tax on the movement because it's debt and can actually get additional phantom income from depreciation.

Q: *So the average person cannot see money moving?*

A: True. All the average person knows is to park their money while people in the I quadrant borrow their money and move it at high speed.

Q: *Is that why so many people say to you, "You can't do that here?"*

A: Yes. I hear it all the time. And that's because most of them are in the E and S quadrants. As these people challenge what we do, I can look out the window and see the large buildings of the people who *are* doing it—*there*.

If you did not understand any parts of this chapter, please find a partner or an accountant and discuss it. It is a very important chapter. If you understand this chapter, you will see what most people never see, even if it is right in front of their eyes.

Chapter Eleven

I QUADRANT:
MASTERS OF MONEY

Poor Dad:
"Go back to school and get your MBA."

Rich Dad:
"Become a Master of Money."

In the spring of 1974, I was flying my last flights with the Marines. Flying between the spectacular islands of Hawaii made leaving the Marine Corps even more difficult. I absolutely loved flying, yet I knew it was time for me to move on.

In June of 1974, I drove off the base, returned the guard's salute for the last time and left for my new life in downtown Honolulu. In a few days, I would start my new life with the Xerox Corporation.

No MBA

My poor dad had wanted me to get my MBA and climb the corporate ladder. I dropped out of the MBA after six months. After flight school and flying for five years, I could not stand the boredom of traditional education.

My dad was disappointed, but he understood. He knew I had come to a fork in the road. He knew I was not going to follow in his footsteps. He knew I was not going to climb a corporate ladder. He knew I wanted to become an entrepreneur.

Skills for an Entrepreneur

My rich dad had suggested I get a job in sales, saying, "The number one skill of an entrepreneur is his or her ability to sell." He would repeatedly say, "Sales = Income" and "If you want more income, sell more."

While still in the Marines, I applied to Xerox because Xerox had the best sales training in corporate America. Soon after being hired, I was flown to Leesburg, Virginia for a four-week sales training program. It was a fabulous four weeks.

I had been in military school and in the military since I was 18 years old. In 1974, at the age of 27, I was finally back in the real world.

The problem was that, even with the best sales training, I was still struggling. I was on the streets of Honolulu, knocking on doors and having doors, literally, slammed in my face. I wasn't making any money because I was not selling. I wanted to quit, but I could hear rich dad's words, "Failing is how you learn in the real world. In the real world you fail until you succeed." So I kept knocking on doors.

Two years later, I was doing a little better. My mind and my body had embraced the salesman's motto: "Selling begins when the customer says 'No.'"

At first, every 'No' hurt. After two years and hundreds of 'Nos,' I actually got excited when the customer said, 'No.' I knew every 'No' meant it was time to start selling. Although I was very shy and terrified of rejection, I actually learned to love selling, I learned to love rejection.

As rich dad taught his son and me:

"Your life transforms, when you learn to love what you fear."

I had learned to love my fear of rejection. Overcoming rejection and turning around a customer's objection became a game.

This works in romance too. All my life, I have been terrible around women. I had no guts. I was a stud flying planes and a wimp around women. Learning to love my fear of rejection changed all that. The first time I saw Kim my old fears came up. She took my breath away. I almost went back to my old behavior and did not ask her for a date.

In 1984, when I asked Kim out, she turned me down. She was polite, but clear she had no interest in me. I got creative (without being obnoxious) and kept asking. She rejected me for six months before she said 'Yes.' We went on our first date and we have been together ever since and recently celebrated our 30th wedding anniversary. I would not be where I am without her. I know she did not marry me for my money because, when we met, I had no money. I was a struggling entrepreneur in the S and I quadrants.

The Best Training for Entrepreneurs

Rich dad was very happy I took a job with Xerox. He said, "Every day you will go to real business school. Every day, you will learn to become a better entrepreneur."

After my second year on the streets, I understood what rich dad was talking about. Every day, my job was to go into a business and study their "paper flow." I had to learn how paper documents flowed from department to department in a business. After studying the paper flow, I could make a more educated recommendation for a new Xerox machine. Studying paper flows allowed me to study many different businesses from the inside out.

Small Entrepreneurs

Since I was a junior sales rep, I was not allowed to sell to major corporate accounts, B-quadrant businesses. I was only allowed to sell to small businesses, run by small entrepreneurs, S-quadrant businesses. Doing business with many different small-business owners was a priceless experience. I came to the conclusion all small business entrepreneurs are crazy. Every one is different, every one a character.

The employees who worked for the entrepreneurs were basically the same, sane and stable. The entrepreneur was frantic and frenetic; a few steps from the funny farm. Their strengths and weaknesses were obvious. And it was obvious their strengths were also their weaknesses. They would never be good employees and they were too independent to grow their business into the B quadrant. I was learning a lot about people, the most important component of a business. I realized most were trapped in the S quadrant.

As my sales (and my income) improved, I knew I was getting closer to the day I would leave the E quadrant. When the company announced that I was #1 in sales, I announced my resignation from Xerox. It was time to move to the S quadrant.

In 1978, I left the E quadrant. My fellow Xerox employees gave me a small going away party. Several said, "You are going to fail and you'll be back." They had seen people like me before. Several Xerox employees had left, failed, and come back.

Smiling and thanking them for four years of friendship, I said, "I know I will fail… but I will never come back."

Transitions

My last day in the E quadrant was my first day in the S quadrant, a day of joy, doubt, terror, and excitement. Two years later, I did fail. I was one of the 9 out of 10 entrepreneurs who fail in their first five years in business. I did lose everything, but I never went back to the E quadrant. I was in deep in S-quadrant hell. There is a saying that goes: *"When you're going through hell… keep going."* That became my mantra.

So I kept going. For years, there were days when I would wake up without a penny in my pocket and employees to pay. By dinnertime, I paid my employees and I had money to pay the company's bills. I was learning another entrepreneurial life skill: How to make money quickly.

The Four Quadrants

Earlier, I presented this diagram, the CASHFLOW Quadrant. Most people go to school and end up in the E quadrant. Most people never leave the E quadrant.

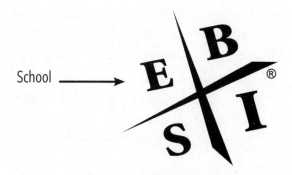

Training for the S Quadrant

A few go to school to gain professional training for the S quadrant. These students go to medical school to become doctors, law school to become attorneys, real estate school to become real estate agents, or trade schools to become electricians or contactors. Having some type of professional education helps when moving from the E quadrant to the S quadrant.

The journey from E to S is very difficult if the entrepreneur has no professional qualification to soften the transition. For example, if an employee quits his job to start a new restaurant, he or she is going to spend some time in S-quadrant hell.

The Right Side of the CASHFLOW Quadrant

Some time in early 1980, I was finally doing well in the S quadrant. My manufacturing company was building products for the surfing industry and the rock and roll industry. The rock and roll division was building licensed-merchandise products for rock bands like The Police,

Duran Duran, Pink Floyd, and Judas Priest. MTV came on the TV scene and pushed our rock and roll business from small to big. We had new problems.

In the beginning, failure nearly killed me. Now success was killing me. I could not keep up with demand. I was constantly raising money and out of money. For example, I would raise money in April to build products. Then I would go on sales trips to sell the products the business was to produce. I promised all my retail customers delivery in October, in time for the holiday season. December would come and go and I'd wait until April for the retailers to pay me. After paying back investors I had to borrow money again for the next holiday season. As I said, success was killing me. I found out success is expensive.

A Visit to Rich Dad

Rich dad was my mentor and coach during this crucial period of my life. I was doing OK in the S quadrant and doing OK in the I quadrant. But I was not setting the world on fire. I was always out of money. I was tired of being poor. I was tired of employees always calling in sick and asking for more money, more time off, and more benefits. I was tired of salespeople who could not sell. I was tired of retail customers wanting lower prices, greater discounts, more "free" products, and longer payment terms. I was tired of government regulations and government inspectors.

S-Quadrant Hell

I was in S-quadrant hell. I was grossing millions of dollars, yet millions of dollars were going out faster than they were coming in.

Rich dad was my coach. I visited him on an irregular basis, generally when I was going through hell. Sitting in his office one night, I told rich dad I wanted to give up. I was tired. I was not successful. I was thinking about going back to flying. I heard the police department was looking for former military pilots to fly for the department. The pay was good, lots of time off, benefits, and government retirement. Just what my poor dad had wanted for me.

Rich dad just laughed. He had known all along that this day would come.

He pulled out his yellow notepad and he drew the CASHFLOW Quadrant with these words in each quadrant:

Mind
Body
Emotions
Spirit
Rules

Rich dad went to explain, "We are all humans, but different beings. All humans have a mind, body, emotions, and spirits. Our differences in mind, body, emotions, and spirits make us different beings."

Most employees do not leave the security of the E quadrant due to the emotion fear. Their fear and need for job security keep them in the E quadrant, even if they know they should leave.

"And right now I am stuck in the S quadrant," I said. "And I can't get out." I asked rich dad, "Is that what you are getting at?"

"Yes," said rich dad, smiling. "You have not yet mastered the S quadrant. The S quadrant is the worst quadrant for many reasons, one being the rules of the S quadrant. Tax rules and government regulations kill small entrepreneurs in the S quadrant."

"Yet, haven't you said, 'The S quadrant is the most important quadrant?'"

"Yes," smirked rich dad. "If you survive." He then asked: "When you were a sales rep for Xerox didn't you see those small business owners fighting for survival?"

"Yes. Everyday. I'm doing the same thing now."

"Always remember a baby learning to walk and a kid learning to ride a bicycle. That is what happens in each and every quadrant. You learned to do well in the E quadrant working for Xerox. Then you moved on to the S quadrant. Today you're a kid riding a bicycle, in the S quadrant, but not going anywhere yet."

I thought about this, then asked him, "My mind, body, emotions, and spirit and have not yet matured in the S quadrant? I have not yet grown up?"

"Correct," said rich dad. "You're doing well. You're close. There are still a few pieces missing. The pieces could be mental, physical, emotional or spiritual—or all of them."

He reminded me that life is like learning to play golf. "In theory golf is a very simple game. Sixty percent of the game is won with a putter and almost everyone can hit a putter. In reality, golf is the toughest game of all. The game is played in our mind, body, emotions, and spirit. The same is true in business. There is nothing outside of you—*everything* is inside," rich dad said.

I left his office confused. I did not know… what I did not know. In my mind, I was doing all the right things. I stopped by a local Chinese restaurant and struggled with my emotions. As I was leaving, the waitress said, "Thank you" and handed me a fortune cookie. Breaking the cookie, I pulled out my fortune, which read:

"You can always quit. Why start now?"

The next morning, I taped my fortune to my telephone—so I would see it every day—and got back to work, dialing for dollars and putting out fires. As the saying goes:

"When you're going through hell, keep going."

Masters of Money—and What They Do

A few months later, I was happier and felt like a human being again. During my coaching session with rich dad, I asked him, "What is the end game? How do I know I've won as an entrepreneur?"

He smiled at me… the smile I had come to recognize—the one that meant he was happy with my question. Taking a breath, he said, "When you reach the I quadrant."

"What happens in the I quadrant?" I asked.

"You become a *Master of Money*. You are no longer a slave to money."

"And what does a master of money do?" I asked.

"Masters of Money do not need money to make money. Masters of Money are alchemists. They turn ideas into gold. They turn ideas into international businesses," rich dad said.

He continued: "And after a person becomes a Master of Money, they do what I am doing with you."

"And what are you doing with me?" I asked.

"I'm guiding you to one day become a Master of Money like me."

"How do I know when I've become a Master of Money?"

"When you develop your Midas touch, when everything you touch turns into gold… in today's world, money."

"Then what do I do?" I asked.

"Then you teach. It is your responsibility to teach, to guide, to develop others like you. The world needs great entrepreneurs. Without great entrepreneurs, the world economy begins to collapse. Capitalism will evolve into socialism, possibly communism… a world of terror, a world of limited freedom, a world of dictators and despots."

"But I have to make it to the I quadrant first, before I can teach?"

"Yes. I think it is better you get to the I-quadrant first. The world is filled with charlatans, false prophets, people who promise to teach you to be rich, but they themselves are not rich. Do not be one of them. Teach from the I quadrant."

Rich Dad's Classroom

I was nine years old when I first sat in rich dad's office. His office was our classroom. At first his office was small, at the back of his first hotel in the small town of Hilo, Hawaii.

By the time I was in my mid-30s, rich dad's office was in a luxury high-rise office building near his massive hotel on Waikiki Beach. I was older and could hear things he could not tell me when I was younger.

"Many people want to be rich, but they take the easy road. Rather than spend time learning and studying—especially about debt, taxes, and phantom income—they do foolish things like cheat, lie, and steal. The world of business is filled with these people. They will say anything, they make promises they never intend to keep, they bend the rules, break the rules then wonder why their reputation is that of a cheat, a sneak, a flim-flam man, a liar, a smooth talker, a BS artist, a con man or woman, a con artist, a dreamer, a bully, a gambler, a two-bit hustler, a petty thief… a person not-to-be-trusted, someone whose word is no good, someone who will trade sex for a raise and promotion. A few do reach the I quadrant but they pay a very high price. The price is their soul."

Looking across his desk at me he said, "Don't be one of them."

The Good News

Rich dad smiled again saying, "The good news is, these people will be your best teachers. They will teach you lessons about yourself even you did not know. They will find your weaknesses and exploit them. They will teach you your weaknesses, the flaws in your thinking and how naïve you are. They will smile at you and pick your pocket at the same time. If you want to learn to do business in the real world, these people will be your best teachers."

Rich dad reminded me of what His Holiness The Dalai Lama said after China invaded Tibet and pushed him out of his temple and home. His Holiness said, "Mao Tse-tung is my best teacher."

Rich dad explained that there are rich people in the E, S, and B quadrants, but they all work for money. The Masters of Money live in the I quadrant. These are rare individuals who do not need money. They can create money out of nothing.

A true master is a teacher, just as a martial arts master is a teacher. Yet, not all people in the I quadrant are teachers. Some use the I quadrant to rule the world. They have the power to buy and sell politicians; they influence elections. They make the rules. They know the golden rule, "He who has the gold makes the rules."

"So you follow the rules of the I quadrant?" I asked.

"Yes," said rich dad. "I follow the rules but I do not have to do what they do. I do have a soul."

Core Values

Rich dad drew the following diagram, explaining the core values of the different *beings* in each quadrant.

"Why does someone in the I quadrant need entrepreneurs?" I asked.

"Because we all need to give back—every one of us. A person in the I quadrant needs to train new entrepreneurs. I need you just as much as you need me. It's Maslow's Hierarchy of Needs. When you reach the top, you give back. If I was a master chef, I would need to train new chefs."

"It's like the old apprentice system," I said.

"Yes, exactly," said rich dad. "Unfortunately today, the ancient apprentice system has been replaced by a government school system, a system that trains employees, not entrepreneurs. That is why we are in trouble as an economy."

Rich dad was concerned. "My son Mike is fortunate. I made the journey through the quadrants for him and I trained him well. As you know, I did not give him anything. That is why the two of you worked for me for free. I am a rich man who started with nothing. I know there is nothing more helpless than the child of a wealthy man. There is nothing more self-destructive than a child born with a sense of entitlement. That is why I treated you both the same. I refused to pay you. I wanted both of you to be humble."

Rich dad had more to tell me: "Humility gives you the ability to see yourself in the context of a much larger world. I wanted you to work with the lowest-paid people at the lowest levels of my business. I wanted you to get to know the workers doing the most humble of jobs. I wanted you to know them as human beings, not just as low-income employees. We are all human beings. That is why I had you do their jobs, working alongside them, doing the same work for free. The people you and Mike worked alongside are the invisible workers in any business. They are the engines of the business. They make the engine of business run. Your job as an entrepreneur, the owner of your business, is to work *for* them. Your most important job is to protect them and their families, from the harsh realities of this world."

Taking a breath, rich dad paused to see if what he said was sinking in with me. When he was certain I heard him, he spoke again saying, "Too many young people with MBAs are people like you, people from middle class families. After getting their Masters degree, they enter a business at the top, the executive level, never knowing the wonderful people at the bottom. Many executives think they are smarter, more intelligent, better than the workers below them. Many lose touch with reality. Many lose touch with their own humanity. To them, employees are just numbers, human beings that can be hired and fired as needed. They fail to realize that all living things rely on each other. No man is a slave to another."

He concluded by saying, "MBAs are trained to lead via numbers, spreadsheets and quarterly reports. They never learn that *kindness* is the greatest trait of a leader. They forget that *manners are not trivial* and *respect is everything*. They work hard, hoping to one day to join the rare few in the I quadrant, but few will make it. It is almost impossible to get from the E quadrant to the I quadrant by avoiding the S and B quadrants. You cannot teach what you do not know. Yet many do."

Rich Kids

Rich dad had some thoughts on rich kids: "Many people in the I quadrant are children of privilege. They grow up rich, in the I quadrant. They come from multi-generational wealth. Their grandparents made their money. They go to expensive, exclusive private elementary and high schools only knowing other children of privilege. Many go on to the finest, most prestigious universities in the world. After graduation, their parents get them positions as apprentices at the top of the corporate and banking worlds, being groomed to one day run the company, without having to start with nothing, without having to learn how to build a business out of nothing, without knowing the real people of the world. It is the ability to build a business out of nothing that makes a person a Master of Money. If you are simply born rich, you may not have what it takes. You are often rich and smart, but out of touch with the real world. And yet, they are the ones who make the rules that make the rich richer, but leave the poor and middle class poorer."

Testing my Humility

"So you were testing my humility before you were willing to teach me?" I asked.

Rich dad only nodded.

"Is that why you had Mike and me do jobs like picking up cigarette butts for free before you were willing to teach us?"

Rich dad nodded, saying, "When you demonstrated your willingness to learn, with humility, I was willing to teach you what I know. If you had said, 'Why should I pick up cigarette butts for free?' I would not have wasted my time teaching either of you. I have more important things to do than to teach two brats how to be rich."

As I left his office that night, rich dad asked, "If you make it to the I quadrant, I want you to promise me that you will teach what I have taught you. If you teach you become a true Master of Money." As I turned to leave he said, "If you teach… then *you, me, and we can change the world from the I quadrant.*"

Good News

Today, due to this global economic crisis, there are many programs on television depicting what real people in the I quadrant do. CNBC, the international financial television channel, has TV programs such as *Shark Tank* and *The Profit*. I love those programs. The "sharks" and "the profit" are doing what real I-quadrant people do. They teach and sometimes finance a business, partnering with future entrepreneurs.

If you have ever watched those programs, you may have noticed one thing that drives the sharks crazy. When a "shark" asks, "What will you do with the money you're looking for?" and the wanna-be entrepreneur says, "I am going to finally pay myself a salary." The sharks check out.

When the wanna-be entrepreneur says, "I've been knocking on doors selling my products and I've sold over a million dollars, and I am now looking for guidance to take the business to the next level," sharks like Mark Cuban or Barbara Corcoran jump up and say, "You're the kind of person I'm looking for."

It was 1983...

In 1983, my rock and roll business was up and running. More money was coming in than going out. The business was finally stabilized. Something inside of me told me that it was time, again, to move on.

That same year, Bucky Fuller passed away on July 1, 1983. A few months later, Fuller's book *Grunch of Giants* was published. After reading *Grunch*, which stands for Gross Universal Cash Heist, I knew it was time to move on. In 1984, I sold my business and decided to become an entrepreneur in education. That same year, I met the most beautiful woman in the world, Kim. In December of 1984, we held hands and took our leap of faith—once again with nothing, once again learning to walk in a new S-quadrant business that tested our mental, physical, emotional, and spiritual intelligences.

Kim and I were following lessons Bucky Fuller had passed on to me. One lessons was, *"I do not work for me, I work for everyone."* Another lesson was, *"Find out what god wants done and do it."* That's what we set out to do.

Kim and I were homeless for a short while. Our spiritual intelligence, our faith, was being tested. Once again, I better understood why rich dad did not pay his son and me. Like true entrepreneurs, Kim and I did not let the lack of money stop us.

We met some horrible people, people who took advantage of us, and our situation. Today, they remain our greatest teachers. We learned a lot about people... and ourselves.

And we met some of the greatest people in the world, people in all parts of the world, people we would never have met if job security was our life's priority.

In 1994, Kim and I made it in the I quadrant. We had $10,000 a month in passive income coming in from real estate investments and only $3,000 in expenses, including a personal mortgage payment. We were free. We had mastered debt, taxes, and phantom income. We no longer needed money. We could create abundance out of nothing. Kim was 37 and I was 47. We celebrated for a week on luxurious Turtle Island in Fiji. The picture below is from Turtle Island, and it was used on the back cover of my book, *Retire Young Retire Rich.*

In 1996, keeping my promise to rich dad, who had since passed away, Kim and I produced the *CASHFLOW* board game.

In 1997, *Rich Dad Poor Dad* was published and in that same year The Rich Dad Company was formed and we began teaching via the B quadrant. We were out of the S quadrant. Our products were now teaching throughout the world.

In 2000, *Rich Dad Poor Dad* made the *New York Times* bestseller list, the only self-published book on the list. That same year, 2000, Oprah Winfrey's guest on *Oprah!* and I learned the power of the Oprah Effect. My world changed overnight.

On February 1, 2004, *The New York Times* ran an article about our board game CASHFLOW stating:

> **"Move over, Monopoly...**
> *a new board game that aims to teach people how to get rich is gaining fans the world over!"*

I kept my promise to rich dad. Today, all across the world in big cities and remote villages, in many different languages, there are thousands of teachers teaching thousands of people the lessons my rich dad taught me, learning by playing the *CASHFLOW* game and reading from Rich Dad books.

As rich dad said, *"You, me and we can change the world from the I quadrant."*

Today, as I-quadrant entrepreneurs, Kim and I invest in entrepreneurs. We do not invest in the stock market. Kim and I invest in S-quadrant entrepreneurs, just as they move to the B quadrant.

The problem with S-quadrant entrepreneurs is most only create lower-paying jobs. For example, a medical doctor employs lower-paid employees. A B-quadrant entrepreneur creates high-paying jobs for CEOs, CFOs, CIOs, and Presidents. When we partner with businesses doing what the government wants done, creating high-paying jobs, providing housing for low income workers, and developing energy, the government becomes our partner by offering us tax breaks.

That is why the people in the I quadrant are the Masters of Money.

Food for the Journey

If you are thinking about leaving your job and starting your own business, or you have already left your job and wanting to move through the quadrants, there are two books I highly recommend. They are:

> *The Miracle Morning* by Hal Elrod
>
> *The Untethered Soul* by Michael Singer

I wish I had these books while I was going through S-quadrant hell. Both books are nonreligious books written for the human spirit. Both books have taught me to get my emotions out of the way and allow my spirit to grow stronger and lead the way.

I have read both of these books twice. Each time I learn more about my spirit. Kim and I have spent many mornings discussing passages from each book. My advisors and I have gathered for three-day study sessions, for in-depth study of both books. That is how important we feel these books are, especially for entrepreneurs.

We have all heard of the *entrepreneurial spirit*. I believe that means that being an entrepreneur is about a spirit, more than a profession.

Chapter Twelve

DO YOU HAVE
A PLAN B?

Poor Dad:

"I am looking forward to retirement."

Rich Dad:

"I retired a long time ago."

My poor dad had a great Plan A. He was an academic genius. He loved school. He did well in school. His plan A was to become a teacher, work for Hawaii's Department of Education, and retire.

Unfortunately, he ran for Lt. Governor as a Republican against his boss, the Democratic Governor of Hawaii, and lost. His plan A did not work. My poor dad had no Plan B.

A New Plan B

Unemployed at the age of 50, poor dad's Plan B was to go into the S quadrant as an entrepreneur. He withdrew his life savings and as well as some government retirement money to purchase a "cannot fail" national ice cream franchise. And the business failed.

He was successful in the E quadrant, but lacked the skills and mindset for the S-quadrant. He simply did not know how to make money as an entrepreneur.

Preparing for the Coming Crisis

Today millions of baby boomers all over the world are in the same predicament that my poor dad was. The crisis will be their retirement. The good news is that most will live longer than their parents did. The bad news is, most will run out of money during retirement.

This is why the creation of the 401(k) in 1978 is significant. The 401(k) shifted the responsibility of an employee's retirement from the employer to the employee. If the employee ran out of money or lost money in a crash, the corporation was no longer responsible to pay the employee a paycheck for life. In 1978, millions of baby boomers suddenly became passive investors… *without* any financial education.

It Gets Worse…

But wait, it got worse. Today with low- to negative-interest rates, printing money, and a stock market bubble, it appears many managed retirement funds are in serious trouble.

Worth repeating here is a quote from Philip Haslam's book, *When Money Destroys Nations,* a book on the collapse of Zimbabwe:

> *"My dad's friend was a partner at a legal firm, having worked there for 50 years. For that entire period he had invested his retirement savings with Old Mutual (the investment company for employees). With hyperinflation, his retirement savings were decimated. Old Mutual sent him a letter saying it wasn't worth paying him monthly, so they paid out the entire amount. With that payment—his entire life's pension—he bought a jerrycan of fuel."*

Q: *Are you saying everyone should have a Plan B?*

A: Yes, especially today. When most people lose their job in the E quadrant, most simply look for another job in the E quadrant. Without financial education, few people ever change quadrants.

In 1973, my Plan A was pretty solid. I was in my mid-20s, had a college degree and two high-paying professions, as a ship's officer and a pilot. I could have returned to Standard Oil and sailed tankers, or flown for the airlines, as many of my fellow Marine pilots did.

Yet my poor dad's unemployment disturbed me. I suspected I was seeing the future, not of my dad's generation, the World War II generation, but of *my* generation, the Vietnam War generation.

Rather than follow my Plan A—sailing or flying professionally— I switched to Plan B and followed in rich dad's footsteps. At the age of 25, my Plan B was to become an entrepreneur in the S quadrant and, at the same time, a professional investor in the I quadrant. My goal was to retire young and never need a paycheck again.

Golden Parachutes

Most public company CEOs have a Plan B. It is called a *golden parachute*. In employment negotiations, Plan B is just as important as Plan A. If the CEO does not do a good job, the CEO simply pulls the ripcord on their Plan-B parachute, often very rich when they leave the company,

Unfortunately, when a CEO does a poor job and *employees* lose their jobs, employees do not have golden parachutes. Employees are lucky to receive pay and benefits for six months.

Wall Street tells you the world economy is getting stronger. Yet, in August of 2016, Cisco announced it would lay off a record number of employees—14,000—representing 20% of its global workforce. These are more than just 14,000 individuals, it's 14,000 families that are affected. I wonder how many of these families have a Plan B.

For millions of people, young and old, their Plan B is go back to school.

"I Ruined My Life"

The August 2016 cover of *Consumer Reports* blares, *"I kind of ruined my life by going to college."* The article was an investigate report on how student loan debt is ruining the lives of millions of people, young and old. Believing in the fairytale of 'a good education,' millions take out loans, go school, and graduate—but are unable to find employment nirvana, and—ironically—leave school learning little to nothing about money.

Today, 42 million Americans owe approximately $1.3 trillion in student loan debt. According to the U.S. Government Accounting Office (GAO) interest on student loan debt is one of the federal government's largest assets. Student loan debt makes the Department of Education one of the biggest banks in America.

Consumer Reports states:

"And in one of the industry's greatest lobbying triumphs, student loans can no longer be discharged in bankruptcy, except in rare cases."

Most school kids and their parents are financially illiterate. A financially illiterate person would not understand what the words *"no longer be discharged in bankruptcy"* means. If anyone ever attempted to get me to sign such a contract, I would toss it back to the educator asking, *"Do you think I'm stupid?"*

Being unable to discharge your loan in bankruptcy makes student loan debt the worst of all types of debt, worst than credit card, mortgage, and business debt. For millions of students, student loan debt will never be forgiven; the student will never be allowed to start over. This is why the cover of *Consumer Reports* gets it right, quoting a student who said, *"I kind of ruined my life by going to college."* Millions of students all over the world are ruining their lives, not only with debt, but by remaining financially illiterate.

The Corruption of Education

For many students today, the price of a good education is too high and the ROI is too low. Today, millions of people, young and old, are leaving school deeply in debt and unable to find that mythical high-paying job for life.

Like it or not, life costs money. Yet we teach students little to nothing about money. Even when students graduate from school, many with advanced degrees, most leave school, financially illiterate. I've asked myself this question thousands of times: *Why is that?*

Little Red Riding Hood

In the story of *Little Red Riding Hood*, the big bad wolf runs ahead of the young girl, to granny's house, eats grandma, puts on grandma's clothes, and waits for Little Red Riding Hood's arrival. This is what the financial services and education industry are doing to students today.

When Little Red Riding Hood says to the big bad wolf, *"What big teeth you have. Why is the cost of education so high?"* The big bad wolf replies, *"With a good education you will get that high-paying job. So, don't worry about the cost of your education. Just sign this 'student loan agreement' and you too will become a college graduate."*

Student loans can never be forgiven, save for rare exceptions. It is the kind of debt banks love. Banks love debt that can never be discharged in bankruptcy. When a student cannot repay their loan the banks have a customer for life.

Who Is Behind Student Loans?

No surprise here. It's the same banks that brought the world the subprime mortgage crisis that are behind the student loan debt crisis.

Giant banks like Citibank and Goldman Sachs, via private equity companies, are funding debt-collection companies for the sole purpose of collecting monthly payments from delinquent students and their parents. The longer the student does not pay, the more money the banks make.

Again, the student loan crisis is an example of financialization and kleptocracy. And financialization cannot occur without *kleptocracy*.

The movie *The Big Short* is about financialization and kleptocracy. Today, the same kleptocracy and financialization that brought you *The Big Short* are active in the business of education.

This is why *Consumer Reports* states:

> *"Today, just about everyone involved in the student loan industry makes money off the students—the banks, private investors, even the federal government."*

Simply put, going to school may not be profitable for students, but student loan debt is very, very profitable for the kleptocracy.

Not Worth the Cost

Consumer Reports states that 45% of those with student loan debt said, *"College was not worth the cost."*

The August 1, 2016 edition of *The Sydney Morning Herald* states, Australia's universities have left many graduates with "broken dreams and a large student debt." The article also states that *"students are being used as cash cows."*

To be fair, if a student can afford a great education, they should. Education is extremely important. Yet, if the long-term cost of education is too high and ROI too low, the student and parents may want to reconsider their options.

I have met two medical doctors who left school, hundreds of thousands of dollars in debt, yet were able to retire their debt because they went on for professional education and did find high-paying jobs.

Students Who Struggle

The students who struggle are students who graduate with a college degree but no professional license. Examples are degrees in art, music, or general science. Today, many college graduates work at jobs that do not require a college degree.

Today, people are recommending going to a trade school to become an electrician, mechanic, or massage therapist, rather than going back to school for a college degree.

Students who fare the worst are those who take out loans and then drop out of school.

Taxing Graduates

Desperate for more money to fund education, England, Ireland, and South Africa are toying with the idea of taxing college graduates. The tax will force college graduates to pay even more for their education, this time funding the college education for future students. Even if they have no student loan debt, they will still be paying for education.

But Wait... It Gets Worse

In the United States, public education is funded by real estate taxes. Due to mismanagement of teachers' union pension funds, many cities cannot afford to pay the pensions of retiring teachers—forcing many cities to raise property taxes. In other words, the homeowner is taxed, to pay teachers' salaries while they are teaching, only to shoulder more taxes to pay for teachers' retirement.

Prices Are Falling

Prices are falling on many of life's expenses such as gasoline, clothing, interest rates, and electronic products... yet the price of education keeps going up. Rising costs of education is another reason why the gap between rich and poor widens. Education is making life more and more expensive for taxpayers, parents, and students. Ironically, *money*, the very subject not taught in schools, is costing all of us a lot more money. Our greatest expense is a world run by highly educated—but financially illiterate—leaders.

My Plan B

As I've said, my Plan A was solid. I could have done very well in the E quadrant as a pilot or ships officer. I loved both jobs. I would have made a lot of money. Yet, if not for my poor dad's Plan A failing, I would not have reconsidered my life's plan.

My Plan B started with real financial education. My Plan B began when I signed up for that 3-day real estate investment course for $385 and I have never looked back. The day I completed the 90-day assignment of looking at 100 properties and writing the one-page evaluations, I was on my way. I knew I would one day make it to the I quadrant.

I did not like high school. For me, school was boring. I was studying subjects that I knew were important, but subjects I had no interest in. When I got to the academy in New York, school became a bit more interesting. I loved sailing ships. And when I got to Navy flight school, I was in heaven. Students would study in the morning and fly in the afternoon. Flight school was my kind of school. It was learning by doing. It was active learning. It was *real* education, not theory.

Transformational Education

We all know a caterpillar crawls for the first part of its life. Then the caterpillar spins a cocoon, and emerges from that cocoon, for the second half of its life, as a butterfly. That is known as metamorphosis, a transformation. *Metamorphosis* means a marked change in appearance, character, condition, or function. I think most people would agree that there is nothing about a caterpillar that would predict a butterfly. If you looked at a caterpillar you might say, "That bug will never fly."

Becoming a Butterfly

That is what happened to me in flight school. That is what happened to me the day I signed up for a three-day real estate course. The day I entered the classroom, I sensed I was about to become a butterfly. I had found my subject and my classroom. I had found my cocoon. I emerged from flight school, three years later, a combat pilot, prepared for the most hostile flying environment in the world: a war zone. I crashed three times in Vietnam and my crew and I survived. We all came back alive.

I emerged from a real financial education program prepared for another hostile environment, the war zone of money. Every time a market crashes, my team and I do more than survive, we emerge richer.

Real Financial Education

My first three-day real estate course was certainly not my last. Kim and I attend seminars on a regular basis. We learn a lot, together, and education makes our marriage stronger. After each seminar we have a lot to talk about. We grow together, rather than grow apart.

My team of Advisors gets together on a regular basis, at least twice a year, to study. Our three days of study is our cocoon. We study books, because the greatest teachers are in books. We study books on business as well as on spirituality. As I've stated earlier, we have studied both *The Miracle Morning* and *The Untethered Soul,* books about the power of the human spirit. Always remember, it is called entrepreneurial *spirit*, not *job*.

Also remember that when a parent says to a child, *"Go to school and get a job"* they are programming their child only for the E quadrant. People like my poor dad get trapped in the E quadrant. When my poor dad attempted to move to the S quadrant, he found out his *being* was still an employee in the E quadrant. At that stage of his life, he did not have the luxury of time, to transform his being, from E to S.

All humans are very different beings. The differences show up in the CASHFLOW Quadrant. Each quadrant is made up of these different intelligences:

Mental Intelligence
Physical Intelligence
Emotional Intelligence
Spiritual Intelligence

Different Rules for Different Quadrants

My poor dad had the mental intelligence of a schoolteacher, not an entrepreneur. He did not speak the language of business or money.

He had the physical intelligence of an employee. He avoided making mistakes.

His emotional intelligence was based on fear—the fear of failing, the fear of not having a job, a steady paycheck, and a government retirement.

And his spiritual intelligence was blocked. His *fears* and *doubts* diminished his spiritual intelligence of *faith* and *trust.*

Moving from E to I is a process of transformation, a metamorphosis, much like a caterpillar becoming a butterfly. There will be painful events along the way. The *being* will be challenged and each challenge is important for the transformation. It's a process; it takes time. It takes willpower and spiritual, mental, emotional, and physical intelligences.

The Master Intelligence

The master intelligence is physical intelligence—humans learn by doing and we are always doing something. (And often we're doing something that may not be good for us.)

Let me ask you a few questions. Have you ever been sitting in class, and your body was there but your mind was gone? Your mind and body were not doing the same things.

Have you ever been reading a book and found your mind wandering… doing something else? Have you ever been talking to someone and you knew they were not listening to you?

The reason I loved flight school was because we studied in the morning and we flew in the afternoon. The moment I strapped into the cockpit of the plane, my physical intelligence took over. My physical intelligence commanded all the other intelligences to pay attention. This was now life and death.

Playing Monopoly

My real financial education began when I was nine. Rich dad, his son, and I played Monopoly together and rich dad explained the real-life financial education behind each move. Later, he would take us to his real green houses and defined further the theoretical lessons we learned playing Monopoly.

My real financial education was much like flight school—*study* and *fly*. In academic education, the master intelligences are mental and emotional, *memorize* and then be *afraid of making mistakes*.

In the real world, *physical intelligence becomes the master intelligence.* Physical intelligence transformed me from a caterpillar into a butterfly, from a poor man into a rich man.

The Cone of Learning

The Cone of Learning, also known as The Cone of Experience, was developed by educational psychologist Edgar Dale in 1946.

After 2 weeks we tend to remember	Cone of Learning	Nature of Involvement
90% of what we say and do	Doing the Real Thing	Active
	Simulating the Real Experience	
	Doing a Dramatic Presentation	
70% of what we say	Giving a Talk	
	Participating in a Discussion	
50% of what we hear and see	Seeing it Done on Location	Passive
	Watching a Demonstration	
	Looking at an Exhibit Watching a Demonstration	
	Watching a Movie	
30% of what we see	Looking at Pictures	
20% of what we hear	Hearing Words (Lecture)	
10% of what we read	Reading	

Source: From Dale. Audio-Visual Methods in Teaching, 1E. © 1969 South-Western, a part of Cengage, Inc. Reproduced by permission. www.cengage.com/permissions

Professor Dale positions reading and lecture at the bottom of the Cone of Learning. At the top are *simulations of the real thing* and then *doing the real thing.*

The primary reason I did well learning from rich dad was because he used simulations—via the game of *Monopoly*—and doing the real thing—visiting his real green houses and understanding the role they played on the path to his red hotel.

The reason my crew and I survived three crashes in Vietnam was because every day during flight school, we simulated in-flight emergencies, including crashing.

One of the most important words in real financial education is the word *practice. Practice*, in the Cone of Learning, is the second line from the top—the words *simulation of the real thing.*

A Real Plan B

A real Plan B must include study and practice. For example, before I purchased my first property, I simulated finding a property 100 times.

For three years I attended courses on investing with stock options. I *paper traded* for three years before I did the "real thing." Today, I love stock market crashes.

In today's volatile world economy, I recommend that everyone have a Plan B, especially for retirement. As stated earlier, the millionaires next door are probably the next to go. Anyone saving money or counting on the stock market or a traditional pension is walking on the edge of financial disaster.

My poor dad had a great Plan A. He did not have a Plan B. He was never able to retire. He worked at odd jobs for the rest of his life. Think about this: Social Security and Medicare saved my poor dad.

Today, Social Security and Medicare are the single-largest unfunded and off-balance-sheet liability of the U.S government, estimated to be between $100 trillion to $250 trillion. What are the changes that the baby-boom generation will be saved?

Observing my poor dad struggling for economic survival taught me a very important lesson. Poor dad inspired me to activate my Plan B immediately. My Plan B allowed me to retire early in life, at the age of 47.

A Five-Year Plan

My friend and mentor, Dr. Alexander Elder, author of the best seller *Trading for a Living* states that it takes about five years and $50,000 to learn to be a professional trader.

I agree. It took me about five years before I became a professional real estate investor. The difference was, it did not take me $50,000 to learn. Learning to become a *real,* real estate professional investor meant learning to use debt, taxes, and phantom income, not traditional money.

Real-world education requires:

- a willingness to learn

- choosing your teachers wisely
  For example be careful who teaches you about money. You do not want someone from the E quadrant teaching you about the I-quadrant.

- practice
  Practice is a most important word. Remember this: professional soccer players practice *five days* for every *day they play*. Musicians *rehearse* for years before becoming rock stars. Doctors and lawyers call their *business a practice*, they practice on you and me.

Practice is the environment where you make mistakes and correct. The more important the lesson, the more you should practice. For example, the closer I got to going to Vietnam, the more my flight crew and I practiced.

Bear in mind that *physical intelligence* is the master intelligence. The moment you start *doing* something, the other intelligences fall in line.

Education's Biggest Mistake

As we've covered in Part One: *Mistakes make the rich richer.* One reason that so many people struggle financially is because they are terrified of making mistakes. Rather than study and practice, they turn their money over to bankers and Wall Street, saving money and investing for the long-term in the stock market, then wonder why they worry about money. Rather than study, practice, and learn… what most millionaires next door are practicing is worrying, complaining, and praying the markets will not crash. That is not an intelligent Plan B.

Kim and I were able to retire early because we had a Plan B. And one purpose of a Plan B is to increase your mental, physical, emotional, and spiritual intelligences so you can change quadrants.

I'll close this chapter with a question: What is your Plan B?

Chapter Thirteen

HOW TO END POVERTY: STUDENTS TEACHING STUDENTS

Poor Dad:
"Give people fish."

Rich Dad:
"Teach people to fish."

The September 2, 2016 issue of *Newsweek* ran a cover story about how growing up poor doesn't just change the way you see the world. It changes your brain. The article stated: "Poverty and the conditions that often accompany it—violence, excessive noise, chaos at home, pollution, malnutrition, abuse and parents without jobs—can affect the interactions, formation and pruning of connections in the young brain."

The article cites numerous studies on the effects of poverty on a child's brain. A few studies went as far as to use MRIs (Magnetic Resonance Imaging) to measure and compare brain sizes between children growing up in poverty to children raised in wealthy families.

A research project, published in 2015, by *Nature Neuroscience*, looked at 1,099 people between ages three and 20 and found that children with parents who had lower incomes had reduced brain surface areas in comparison to children from families with household incomes of $150,000 or more a year.

The conclusion of most researchers was that it was more than just money that was the problem—it was growing up in environments of crime, violence, drugs, gangs, promiscuity, and single-parent households that were the real problems. It was living in chronic fear, physical as well as financial, that stunted brain development.

The study showed that if parents, even poor parents, provided a safe, nurturing environment at home, a child had a better chance of normal brain development—even if the neighborhood was violent.

The *Newsweek* article states:

> *"Housing discrimination against minorities living in unsafe, dilapidated buildings, implicit racial bias by teachers, malnutrition, and underfunded schools in poor communities can hamper normal brain development."*

Some Good News

Newsweek goes on to state the brain can change. The damage caused by early childhood poverty can be reversed. The article states:

> *"The brain's neuroplasticity—its ability to modify its own structure—is highest around birth and early childhood, and it decreases over time, but never to zero.*
>
> *"And between the ages of 15 to 30 the brain undergoes a second spurt of increased neuroplasticity, which means that adolescents and young adults, with coaching and practice, are primed to adapt."*

Boys and Girls Clubs

In early 2000, a group of students—young adults from our entrepreneur program, decided to "Pay It Forward" and put what they learned into action. They went to the Boys and Girls Club of South Phoenix, a tough gang-ridden community, and taught students and their parents entrepreneurial lessons I had taught them.

The club is fenced, in order to keep the OGs (Old Guys) out. The OGs are recruiters looking for future pushers, pimps and prostitutes.

It is a terrifying environment to grow up in. The Boys and Girls Club provided a safe haven, even if just for a few hours.

For two months, my students taught a course on entrepreneurship and investing, using the *CASHFLOW* game as the centerpiece of their training program. Their students were young people, ages 12 to 18, and their parents.

The results were transformational. As the *Newsweek* article states, between the ages of 15 and 30, the brain goes through another increase in neuroplasticity. Everyone was amazed when one boy, about 15 years old—a boy people had labeled "cognitively challenged"— suddenly came to life. He had struggled with comprehending what he read. But playing *CASHFLOW* was a whole different thing. The lights in his brain went on! He could not stop playing the game. He could read the cards. He could do the math. He understood the difference between assets and liabilities. He would run to the club just to attend the class and play *CASHFLOW*. A reminder that physical intelligence is the master intelligence. He was not responding to just *reading* a book, which was why he was labeled cognitively impaired. Playing the board game required him to learn physically, reading, computing and understanding financial terms, doing the math using a pencil, moving his game piece, and interacting socially with the other players. Every time that young man physically played *CASHFLOW*, all of his intelligences were engaged.

Many of the parents went through their own transformations. They formed a club and began investing in silver coins. Eventually the parent-student club got permission from the Boys and Girls Club to buy a vending machine. Unfortunately, the vending machine sold soft drinks—and this was a group that did not need any more sugar. Apart from that, the business lesson was important. The group shared their profits with the Club.

That two-month project shifted the parents, students, and faculty from the E quadrant to the S quadrant (with their vending machine) and to the I quadrant (with their personal investments in silver coins).

Members of the student-parent group used copies of financial statements from the *CASHFLOW* game and filled in their own "real numbers." The learning process followed the Cone of Learning, going from *simulation* to *doing the real thing*.

There were many heart-to-heart discussions, as parents and students realized they were focused only on income and expenses, rather than assets and liabilities. I could sense changes were going on inside— mentally, physically, emotionally, and spiritually—for both parents and students.

St. Andrew's College, South Africa

In 2015, Kim, three of her girlfriends, and I traveled to Grahamstown, South Africa, a city that has hosted festivals for 180 years, for the National Arts Festival.

I am unable to describe the beauty of Grahamstown or the magic of the National Arts Festival. The best I can do to describe Grahamstown and the NAF is as a cross between Beatrix Potter and Harry Potter. I thought I had gone back in time, to a time when life was peaceful, idyllic, and magical.

Grahamstown is an academic town of approximately 70,000 residents. It is home to Rhodes University, named after Cecil Rhodes the founding force behind the Rhodes Scholarship.

Grahamstown is also home to St. Andrew's College, an Anglican school for boys, founded in 1855. Today, it is a full boarding school, with 450 high-school-age boys from all over the world. Its sister school is the Diocesan School for Girls.

A friend, Murray Danckwerts, has two boys who attend St. Andrews. For years he has raved about what a fine school it is. One day, he told me about an outreach program sponsored by the school. The program encourages their students of privilege to go into the African township that surrounds Grahamstown to teach less fortunate students. It is a program of students teaching students, and students being taught the importance of *paying it forward*, which is a key component in the educational program at St. Andrew's.

When I heard about this outreach program, I asked Murray if he could approach the school and offer to teach their students financial education, using the *CASHFLOW* game.

The school accepted my offer and in July of 2016, Tom Wheelwright and I traveled to Grahamstown, at our expense, and put on a two-day workshop.

The Difference

The difference was in the diversity of the group we assembled. I asked St. Andrews to include students—both boys and girls, white and black—and instructors from St. Andrew's and Rhodes University, as well as Murray's friends, B- and I-quadrant entrepreneurs from the Grahamstown area in the two-day class.

The reason for having teachers as well as B- and I-quadrant entrepreneurs participate with students is because we all know many business people complain about the lack of real-world exposure of many students. Having school faculty and entrepreneurs working together as teachers would give the 43 high-school-age students an expanded reality of the real world of business.

A Magical Event

The two-day event was magical. The students were fabulous as were the teachers and entrepreneurs. I saw the same lights going on—for the students, teachers, and entrepreneurs—as the awakening I had witnessed at the Boys and Girls Club in Phoenix.

At each table were four to five students and an instructor or a local entrepreneur. After brief introductions from Tom and me, the playing of the game of *CASHFLOW* began.

The First Hour...

The first game was played for one hour. That hour was painfully slow, a bit of a struggle as the adults and students learned the vocabulary, math, and processes taught in the game. Although the game was not finished in the first hour, it was put away and discussion began.

If you will take another look at Dr. Edgar Dale's Cone of Learning on page 209, you will see that participating in a discussion is very high on the retention of learning. Students, teachers, and entrepreneurs had a lot to say after just an hour of game play! The learning was beginning.

The Second Hour

After lunch, the *CASHFLOW* game was played for the second time, and again only for one hour. This time the play had picked up speed. The lights were going on and the second discussion was much more vigorous and in-depth.

The Next Day...

The third hour of play commenced the following morning. This time the game was almost out of control. The noise level had gone up. There was no doubt that both adults and students were "into the game." The third round of discussion was loud and animated—as more and more participants experienced "lights going on" in their brains.

The interesting thing was rather than people saying to Tom Wheelwright, "You can't do that here in Africa," the local entrepreneurs said, "We are doing it here."

The two-day program came to an end as Tom and I presented real-life problems to solve, problems such as "How buying a Porsche can make you richer." The young boys especially liked that problem, just as I thought they might. Again, my joy was in seeing the lights of adults and students going on... and *staying* on.

The Aftermath

Murray called me a few days after the event and said his phone had been ringing hot. He said parents were calling, wanting to know what happened to their child. One boy called his dad and asked to borrow 100,000 rand (South African currency) to invest in his first property. Obviously, he was asked to study the subject of real estate further. Other students were getting together to start their first businesses.

St. Andrew's College is a leader in education. They are forward thinkers. They think big. The leaders of St. Andrew's, along with faculty and the local entrepreneurs, are getting together to discuss how real financial education can be implemented in St. Andrew's as well as in the African township, with students of privilege teaching less fortunate students. *Paying it forward* is alive and well in magical Grahamstown, South Africa.

This book is dedicated to the students, faculty, and entrepreneurs who participated in the two-day program in July of 2016, hosted by St. Andrew's College.

For Tom Wheelwright and me, acting as catalysts amongst students, faculty, and entrepreneurs, was a spiritual event. Ask any teacher how it feels to see "lights going on" for his or her students and you will know why teachers teach.

Spiritual Education

My spiritual education began in August of 1965. After a year of competitive exams and interviews, I received a Congressional nomination to the U.S. Naval Academy at Annapolis, Maryland and the U.S. Merchant Marine Academy at Kings Point, New York.

I accepted the appointment to Kings Point, because I wanted to sail the world as an officer in the U.S. Merchant Marine, not as a Naval officer. Also a consideration in that decision was the fact that King Pointers were among the highest paid graduates in the world, at that time. In 1969, many of my classmates were taking jobs as officers on merchant ships paying over $100,000 a year, which was a lot for a 21-year-old in 1969.

Ironically, I activated my commission as a U.S. Marine 2nd Lieutenant and went to flight school in Pensacola, Florida, with starting pay of $200 a month. I volunteered to fight in Vietnam because of the spiritual education students receive at military academies.

It may sound strange to hear that military academies teach spiritual education, yet they do. The first word taught at all military schools is "mission." The next words were duty, honor, code, respect, and integrity… all words of spiritual literacy.

One of the reasons I dropped out of my MBA program was because the words I was learning in that program were very different:

money, markets, and manipulation. As I stated earlier, I was still in the Marine Corps while in the MBA program. Having just returned from Vietnam, the words money, markets, and manipulation violated the code of honor that had been instilled at the Academy and in the Marine Corps.

Justice

There is one thing every military officer has no patience for: injustice. At the academy and in the Marine Corps, military officers are trained to fight for human dignity at all times.

Returning from Vietnam in 1973, finding my dad unemployed and his spirit crushed, I found my next mission. That mission would one day become The Rich Dad Company mission: to elevate the financial well-being of humanity, via financial education.

To the students and faculty of St. Andrew's College, The Diocesan School for Girls, and Rhodes University, and the entrepreneurs of Grahamstown, thank you for inspiring me to write this book. I especially thank all of you for carrying on the spirit of "paying it forward," which is the true mission of real education.

What IS Real Education?

Real education should *inspire*. It should touch the student's spirit.

Real education should also *encourage*. The word *courage* is derived from the French word *la coeur*, the heart, the ability to overcome the emotions of fear and doubt.

Real education should *empower*. It should give the student the ability to operate effectively, making a difference in the real world.

Real education should *enlighten*. Real education should open the student's mind to the wonders of this world and make them a student for life.

Part Three

SUMMARY

The baby-boom generation is the luckiest generation in history.

They were born at the end of World War II, just as the world economy was set to boom. Even if a baby boomer did not go to college, there were plenty of high-paying jobs.

College-graduate boomers did find jobs that turned into high-paying careers.

Savers Were Winners

With interest rates over 15%, baby boomers could actively save money and become rich.

The suburbs boomed and many boomers paid off their credit card debt by refinancing their homes or became rich flipping McMansions.

Many boomers got rich riding the stock market boom from 1971 to 2000.

A Whole New World

Times have changed. The children and grandchildren of baby boomers face an entirely different world.

What does a person do in a world of accelerating globalization, lower-paying jobs, low interest rates, dangerously high government debt, rising taxes, and rising bureaucratic incompetence?

This is when real financial education becomes vital, not just for success, but for economic survival.

Real financial education requires that we look at all three sides to the coin of money.

Debt and Taxes

Real financial education must be about debt and taxes. Debt and taxes are our greatest expenses. It is naïve as well as ignorant to believe that "Paying taxes is patriotic."

America was born out of a tax rebellion, in 1773. America was basically a tax-free nation until 1943, when the Current Tax Payment Act was passed. The Current Tax Payment Act gave the government permission to put their hands into the pockets of all workers to pay for World War II. This is why so many people believe paying taxes is patriotic. Today taxes feed the Warfare State of America *and* the Welfare State of America.

Today's Reality

Real financial education must be about being an *employee in the E quadrant* to gain real world experience, as well as an *entrepreneur in the S quadrant,* having a part-time business, as well as a *professional investor in the I quadrant.*

It is not enough, and financially ignorant, to simply say, "I have a job."

Real financial education is not about mindlessly turning your money over to a "financial expert" and expecting that money to be there when you need it.

Build Your Team

It is foolish to think you can solve financial problems on your own. The rich have the best accountants and attorneys working for them, solving their problems.

You can do the same. All my personal Advisors have written their own books to support you and your real financial education.

To mindlessly save money, invest for the long term in the stock market, or count on a government pension for financial security will be financial suicide in the future.

A Team of Specialists

The biggest challenge for someone in the S quadrant is that they are smart. I get it. I was always the A student. What happens is that because they are smart, they can do everything. They can do the sales, the marketing, the production, the administrative work. They can even develop the product. This is what keeps them in the S quadrant—and out of the B and I quadrants.

They don't see a need for a team and believe that the team could never do "it" as well as they can. They simply do not trust others to do their job. If you want to move to the B and the I quadrants, you need smart people on your team who are better and more specialized than you are—and you need to trust them to do their jobs.

One of the most frequent questions I am asked is how to find good advisors. Whether it's a tax advisor, financial advisor, or legal advisor, the key will be their understanding of money and their level of education. For a tax advisor, here is the range of education. The more education, the better the advisor.

The More Educated the Advisor the Better the Advice

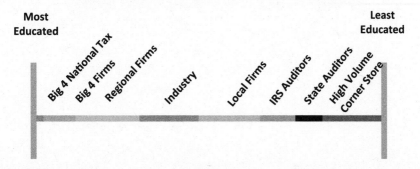

225

Part Four

NO FUN
ECONOMICS

Introduction to Part Four

LIFE IN THE FAST LANE

Most financial experts say the same thing: "Study hard, work hard, pay your taxes, live below your means, save money, eat at home, pay your bills, live debt free, and drive cheap cars."

I call this **No Fun Economics**.

When Tom Wheelwright and I went to teach at St. Andrew's College and The Diocesan School for Girls in South Africa, we taught the way I was taught—by playing games, with real teachers and real entrepreneurs as teachers, and using real examples of how I got rich.

In many of my talks, I often say, "I may be Japanese, but I do not look good in Toyotas. I look better in Corvettes, Porsches, and Ferraris."

At the two-day seminar for students in Grahamstown, I used a real life example of how buying a Porsche made me richer.

The students were much more receptive to Porsche Economics than No Fun Economics.

The following chapter is the same example we studied with the students in South Africa. One of the advantages of a real financial education is you can have fun, live above your means... and still get richer.

Chapter Fourteen

How a Porsche Can Make You Richer

Poor Dad:

"Live below your means."

Rich Dad:

"Expand your means."

Money breaks up many marriages. More couples fight about money than any other subject.

As a young boy, I remember the pain I felt listening to my mom and dad fight about money. That was not the kind of marriage I wanted. I wanted a rich, happy, and loving marriage.

The Vow

A vow is a solemn promise you make before god.

When Kim and I decided to get married, one of the vows we made to each other was this:

> *We could have anything we wanted. But rather than say, "We can't afford it," Kim and I vowed to work together to be able to afford anything she or I or we wanted.*
>
> *There was one condition. That condition was, we had to first purchase an asset and that asset would pay for the liability we wanted.*

In other words, we vowed that the liability would make us richer, not poorer.

The Porsche Problem

This is where the problem of the Porsche came from. This Porsche problem was the same one Tom and I presented to the students of St. Andrew's College and The Diocesan School For Girls, in Grahamstown.

I am a car nut. Kim is not. For years I wanted a 1989 Porsche Speedster. The problem was, they were very rare and very expensive. I believe there were fewer than 700 shipped to America. Rich guys were buying the cars and putting them up on blocks, waiting for the prices to go higher. At one time, I saw one come up for sale for $120,000.

Then the bottom fell out of the economy and Porsche Speedster prices started to come down.

One day, my friend Gary, the Porsche dealer, called and said, "I have the car you have been waiting for. It is the rarest of all 1989 Porsche Speedsters."

"Why is it the rarest?" I asked.

"Because it is Speedster #1, the first 1989 Speedster ever produced. It was the car on the cover of the Porsche catalogue. It was the car that Porsche showed at the major car shows all over the world. I have all the records, catalogues, and plaques commemorating this very special car."

"How much?" I asked, hoping he would say $120,000… to which I would say, "Thanks, but no thanks." The year was 1995 and I was still building up my asset column, and had no room for a car.

"You won't believe this," Gary said. "The owner only wants $50,000."

"What?" I gasped. "What is wrong with the car?"

"Nothing," said Gary. "My mechanics went over the car yesterday, and everything is perfect. And it only has 4,000 miles on the odometer. I am calling you first. If you say 'No,' I will sell it to someone else, today. I have a long list of people who want this car, especially at this price."

One of the things rich dad taught me was to *buy, inspect, and then reject*. Rich dad said, "Most people reject without buying the time to think, to figure things out." In the vocabulary of money, it is called *optioning*, I bought the option, the time to think, before buying the Porsche.

So I told Gary, "I'll take it."

Now I had to figure out how to sell the idea of a new Porsche to Kim.

The Vow... Revisited

And this is where the vow between Kim and I kicked in. All I had to do was buy *an asset* that would give us the cash flow to offset the purchase of my Porsche, *the liability*.

This is the same challenge—the Porsche problem—that Tom and I presented to the students in Grahamstown. Obviously, they were more excited about learning how to buy a Porsche than how to live below their means, save money, and drive a cheap car.

KISS: Keep It Super Simple

I will present the Porsche challenge in the same way I presented it to those young people. Keep in mind that the numbers have been rounded off and the steps simplified for an understanding of the process. An additional note: the numbers on both the Porsche and the mini-storage are low because both were purchased during a crash in the economy.

The Porsche challenge will be presented in three levels.

Level One: The marriage vow

Level Two: Robert's level

Level Three: Tom's level

Level One is the level I used to pitch the Porsche deal to Kim.

Level Two is the level I used to put the deal together.

Level Three is Tom's professional level of thought. I do not fully understand Tom's level, but Kim must have Tom's blessing for the deal to work.

Truthfully, I still do not fully understand how buying a Porsche made Kim and me richer—at least not at the level Tom does. That is why he has his own level.

Every time Kim and I test our marriage vow, Tom expands his role from accountant to marriage counselor, guiding me and Kim through the process. Not only do Kim and I get everything we want, but we get richer and smarter in the process. And it sure beats arguing about money.

Level One: The Marriage Vow

Kim and I had $50,000 in cash in the bank. We could have paid for the Porsche in cash. The problem was, we would then have a Porsche, but no asset and no cash.

INCOME STATEMENT

Income
Expenses

BALANCE SHEET

Assets	Liabilities
$50,000 cash	

The solution?

Find an asset.

Use the $50,000 as a down payment on an asset.

Use debt plus the $50,000 to buy the asset.

Borrow $50,000 to buy the Porsche.

The cash flow from the asset would make the monthly payments on the loan for the Porsche. And when the Porsche was paid off in a few years, Kim and I would own the Porsche *and* the asset, plus the cash flow from the asset.

We would also receive phantom income from appreciation, depreciation, and amortization of the Porsche and the investment.

When Kim understood the Porsche Plan, I proceeded to put the real deal together.

Level Two: Robert's Level

Step one was find an asset. Without a great asset, the deal would not work. In fact, it would backfire, costing more money than I would have saved.

I started calling real estate entrepreneurs I knew and asking if they had anything that might fit what I was looking for.

After five or six calls, a friend in Austin, Texas named Bill said he was just finishing a mini-storage, a mini-warehouse, investment. The mini-storage had been in foreclosure, Bill had purchased it for about $140,000, made some improvements, and would sell it to me for $250,000. The deal was perfect. I trusted Bill, having done a number of deals with him in the past, so I bought the mini-warehouse. A week later, I took out two loans—one for the Porsche and one for the mini-warehouse.

The transaction looked like this:

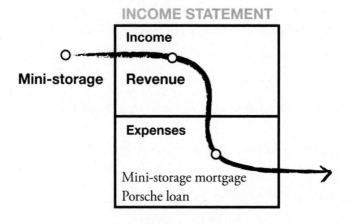

The deal was complete. The cash flow from the mini-warehouse was paying off the Porsche and the mortgage on the mini-warehouse.

I had an asset, I was making more money, paying less in taxes, and driving the Porsche of my dreams.

We sold the mini-warehouse a number of years ago, made a nice profit, and reinvested the profits tax-free. And I still own the Porsche.

Level Three: Tom's Level

Between his command of the tax law and his understanding of both the goals and challenges of entrepreneurs, it isn't surprising that Kim and I believe we've found the perfect partner in Tom related to taxes and wealth strategies. Here's a tax strategist's explanation of the process

Tax Lessons from Tom

Accounting for the Porsche

What Robert describes very simply is precisely what happened when he first acquired the warehouse and then acquired the Porsche. Here are the accounting entries I would use to show the steps of this transaction and the fact that Robert's net worth went up by $1,100 in the first month of owning the Porsche. He started with $50,000 of cash and a $50,000 net worth. After one month of owning the Porsche, his net worth was $51,100.

Follow me through these steps:

Step 1: Purchase the Warehouse

Cash	Warehouse	Mortgage
$50,000	$250,000	$200,000

$50,000 of cash used for the down payment on the warehouse

Step 2: Monthly net income from the warehouse

Cash	Rent	Mortgage Payment	Expenses
$1,000	$2,700	$1,200	$500

$2,700 in rent revenue pays expenses plus mortgage—with $1,000 in positive cash flow left over

Step 3: Purchase the Porsche

Car Loan	Porsche
$50,000	$50,000

$50,000 car loan recorded as a liability; $50,000 Porsche added to asset column

Step 4: Pay monthly car loan

Car Loan	Cash
$1,000	$1,000

Again, if you do not fully understand this explanation, discuss these levels with a friend or find a person like Tom and have them explain the process to you.

Real Teachers, Real Lessons

The students loved this real life example. One by one, students would stand and "walk through" the thought process, explaining to the group how buying a Porsche made me richer, not poorer.

As the students took turns, going through the "process," Tom and I could see the change. We could see it in their eyes… as "the lights were going on." By the end of the two-day seminar, students understood why a financial statement was important for anyone who wanted to have a Porsche make them richer. Many realized they could not use their banker's money if their financial statement, their real-life "report card" when they left school, was not impeccable.

Tom and I did not have to cajole, threaten, harangue—or even encourage—them to learn more. Most, although not all, *wanted* to learn more. Many went over the stack of Rich Dad Advisor books we had stacked on a table nearby, and I encouraged them to read the ones that interested them. The books were free. All Tom and I asked was that they "pay it forward"—passing on what they learned when they went into the African township to teach the CASHFLOW game to other students. It was Tom who said, "The smarter you are, the smarter your African friends will be. Pay it forward."

Life-Long Learning

For millions of people, their education ends when they leave school. For many people, traditional education kills their spirit of learning. This is a socio-economic tragedy.

If not for my rich dad I would have been one of those people.

Inspiring me to become an entrepreneur—not for money, but for personal freedom—he taught me that learning to sell was my entry into the B quadrant. And taking a 3-day real estate course was my entry into the I-quadrant.

The love of learning and lifelong education are essential for success in the B and I quadrants. Today, Kim, my advisors and I get together twice a year to study great books written by great teachers. The world is moving way too fast for us to stand still.

For most people, their education ends when they leave school. That is the primary reason why the gap between the rich, the poor, and the middle class grows wider.

Part Four

SUMMARY

There are few things in life that are as powerful as doing the real thing. Some call it *experiential learning*. And it's at the very top of the Cone of Learning as the most effective way to retain what we learn.

If you look at the Cone of Learning again, I think you can better understand what happened during those two days in Grahamstown.

Cone of Learning

After 2 weeks we tend to remember		Nature of Involvement
90% of what we say and do	Doing the Real Thing	Active
	Simulating the Real Experience	
	Doing a Dramatic Presentation	
70% of what we say	Giving a Talk	
	Participating in a Discussion	
50% of what we hear and see	Seeing it Done on Location	Passive
	Watching a Demonstration	
	Looking at an Exhibit Watching a Demonstration	
	Watching a Movie	
30% of what we see	Looking at Pictures	
20% of what we hear	Hearing Words (Lecture)	
10% of what we read	Reading	

Source: From Dale. Audio-Visual Methods in Teaching, 1E. © 1969 South-Western, a part of Cengage, Inc. Reproduced by permission. www.cengage.com/permissions

When the students played the *CASHFLOW* game three times, for an hour each time, they were at level two: simulation. When they explained my Porsche challenge, they were explaining the real thing.

Once they understood the power of real financial education, the power of the Porsche and the ability to live the life of their dreams and teach others, they were more interested in the bottom level of the Cone of Learning—reading. Many were more willing to read and attend more classes on real financial education.

I know the Cone of Learning process works, because it illustrates the same learning process my rich dad used to teach his son and me. When we were nine years old, we played Monopoly, worked in rich dad's office and went to visit his real "green houses," houses that would one day become a big red hotel.

As I've written about in *Rich Dad Poor Dad*, rich dad's refusal to pay us forced me to think like an entrepreneur and start my comic book business at the age of nine. As the Cone of Learning shows us, nothing is better than doing the real thing. At the age of nine, my comic books were putting money in my pocket—without me working—and I had learned the difference between an *asset* and a *liability*. Those simple lessons have made all the difference in my life.

Today, Kim and I are real entrepreneurs. We do not work for money, we create assets, create jobs, and play Monopoly in real life. And we partner with the government doing what the government wants done and, in exchange, the government gives us tax incentives to be good partners.

Most importantly, we surround ourselves with great friends and advisors. We know business, investing, and life are team sports.

After achieving financial freedom in 1994, Kim and I created the *CASHFLOW* board game in 1996. In 1997, *Rich Dad Poor Dad* was published. All we were doing was "paying it forward" and supporting the mission of The Rich Dad Company:

to elevate the financial well-being of humanity.

This book, *Why the Rich Are Getting Richer,* is really Rich Dad Graduate School. Its release, in 2017, celebrates the 20th anniversary of *Rich Dad Poor Dad.* Kim and I thank all the people all over the world who are playing the *CASHFLOW* game, reading, teaching, sharing, and "paying it forward."

As Margaret Mead once said:

> *"Never doubt that a small group of thoughtful,*
> *committed, citizens can change the world.*
> *Indeed, it is the only thing that ever has."*

FINAL WORDS

Poor Dad:
"Give a man a fish."

Rich Dad:
"Teach a man to fish."

Obviously, our current education system is obsolete. It was designed for the Industrial Age.

The good news is that we are in the Information Age, an age with greater opportunity for more people. While it is true that technology is taking away jobs from traditional employees, it is also creating very rich entrepreneurs who are creative, ambitious, cooperative, and invest in real financial education. In the next 20 years, it will be the tech-savvy entrepreneurs who will change the world—not our schools, government bureaucrats, corporate executives, or politicians.

The biggest mistake most people make is that they believe the next 20 years will be like the past 20 years. Many believe we will soon get through this rough patch in the economy and everything will be OK again.

Like it or not, we are going through the most dramatic change in human history. The clichés, *tectonic plates are moving* and *our tomorrows will not be our yesterdays,* are words of wisdom worth heeding. The question is: Will our current educational system change with our evolution, or will it lead us to our extinction?

Education is more important than ever before, but the pressing question is: What kind of education?

Without real financial education, it is understandable why millions of honest people become tax cheats, doing dishonest deeds and hoping to make a "few bucks under the table," without paying taxes. That is *tax evasion* and it is a criminal act.

Without real financial education, most people do not know the difference between *tax evasion,* which is illegal, and *tax avoidance,* which is legal.

Without real financial education, it is understandable why many people believe the best way to pay less taxes is *to work less—or not work at all.*

Without real financial education, most people do not realize the Federal Reserve Bank and the U.S. Tax Department are related, created in the same year, 1913.

Without real financial education it is understandable why people believe in taxing the rich as a solution to their personal financial problems.

Without real financial education, it is easy to understand why so many people lie to cover the mistakes they make, rather than be truthful and learn from their mistakes.

Millions of people would rather lie about their personal financial condition than admit they know little about money, and then seek help. Without a real financial statement or financial literacy, most people do not really know how threatening their financial challenges are.

At a time when truth and transparency are critical, our schools teach students that mistakes mean you are stupid and, in business, mistakes can mean, "You're fired."

We have become a dysfunctional culture where lying is the best solution for self-preservation.

Since the lack of real financial education is the real problem, then it follows real financial education is the way out.

In closing, the most important question for you to consider is: What do you really want...*really?*

Do you want job security or financial freedom? The answer to that question will determine the type of education that is best for you.

The best words of wisdom for this period of human evolution, in my opinion, come from F. Scott Fitzgerald:

> *"The test of a first-rate intelligence is the ability to hold two opposing ideas in mind at the same time and still retain the ability to function."*

Thank you for reading this book.

Robert Kiyosaki

AFTERWORD

So… how do we change the world?

Rich dad often said: *"If you want to change the world, start by changing yourself."*

Whenever I was complaining or whining about something, he would have me repeat to myself:

"For things to change… first I must change."

He wanted me to think about how *I* could change. I would report back to him when I had new ideas. I was always surprised how things changed, once I made changes.

A MESSAGE TO MILLENNIALS

The Baby Boomers have had a very easy life.
They are not your best financial advisors.

More than half of all baby boomers will retire in poverty.
It's likely many will live with their kids… and grandkids.

You have two choices:
either the government will take care of you…
or you can take care of yourself.

You can fish… or be given fish.
The choice is yours.

BONUS SECTIONS

GRADUATE SCHOOL

A REAL INFINITE-RETURN DEAL
WITH RICH DAD ADVISOR KEN MCELROY

The Project
Forest Ridge Apartment House
Location: Flagstaff, Arizona

267 Units   (50/50 split between 1- and 2-bedroom units)
Price: $19 million

Description: A 30-year-old apartment complex in sound condition, in
need of only exterior, "cosmetic" work

The Opportunity
Flagstaff is a beautiful, small mountain community next to a ski resort,
a state university, and a community college.

Flagstaff is too small for REITs (Real Estate Investment Trusts) that
tend to invest only in larger cities such as Los Angeles and Phoenix.
This gives small investors a chance for great deals.

Flagstaff is a "Pro Green," or anti-growth community, which keeps new
development out. Consequently, homes and apartments are in high demand.

Rents were under market by $100 per month per unit.
Rents could increase gross income by 267 units x $100 soon after
acquisition of the property.

Acquisition Plan

Purchase price: $19 million

Debt: $15 million bank loan

Equity: $4 million equity from seven investors

Added Value Plan

Improve property

Slowly raise rents to market value

Increase NOI (Net Operating Income*)

Refinance the property

Investors get back equity + share of increased value + plus cash flow + tax breaks

	2009	2010	2015
Property value	$19 million	$25 million	$34 million
Debt	$15 million	$20 million**	$25 million**
Equity	$4 million	$5 million	$9 million
NOI	$1 million	$1.4 million	$1.8 million
Cash Flow Before Tax	$400K	$600K	$400K
Tax Benefits (Phantom income)	$675K	$675K	$450K

Note: All numbers referenced above are rounded and approximate for simplicity.

2009

Kim and Robert put in $500,000 of the $4 million equity raise for 12.5% interest. Non-taxable cash flow of $50,000/year was paid out to them. Tax benefits of $84,000 received by them by way of taxes they did not have to pay on other income they earned. Return on Investment (ROI) after taxes was 27 percent.

2010

After an increase in NOI, Ken McElroy refinanced and received a $20 million loan. That loan paid off the prior $15 million loan on the property. All investors received their $4 million in equity plus a portion of the increased (NOI* $1.4) value of the property.

Kim and Robert received their $500,000 back plus $100,000 of increased property value tax-free because the money is debt from a refinance.

ROI (Return on Investment) is now infinite, since Kim and Robert no longer have their own money in the property.

In addition, they received their share of the $600,000 in tax-free cash flow, plus approximately $80,000 a year in tax benefits due to depreciation.

2015

The economy recovered and rents increased, increasing the NOI* to $1.8 million.

Plus, interest rates on loans went down under 5%. Ken McElroy went back to the bank for a loan of $25 million based on a $34 million appraisal of the property.

Again, he paid off the $20 million loan and shared proceeds with the investors.

Kim and Robert received another $500,000 in tax-free proceeds, plus tax-free cash flow of approximately $100,000 as well as phantom income from the tax benefits of depreciation of over $50,000.

Again: their ROI** is infinite.

From 2009 through 2015, Forest Ridge Apartments returned several millions of dollars, tax free—and an infinite return… money from knowledge. That's real financial education.

Over the years, Kim and Robert have invested in 16 similar projects—all with infinite returns—with Ken McElroy and his company, MC Properties.

In most cases, when Ken returns money to Kim and Robert they immediately return the money to Ken to reinvest in other projects that use the same infinite-return model.

Reinvesting returns is another reason why the rich keep getting richer.

Definitions
*NOI: Net Operating Income

		Gross Income from property
Minus	-	Operating expenses (no debt)
Equals	=	**Net Operating Income**

Note: Banks value a property on NOI, Net Operating Income
Every time Ken McElroy increased the NOI, he went back to the bank to refinance the property. Since debt is tax free, the proceeds are distributed to investors… tax free.

**ROI: Return On Investment

$$\frac{Equity}{Return}$$

For example: If I put $100 into an investment and I receive $10 back, my ROI is 10%.

$$\frac{\$100}{\$10} = 10\%$$

If I have 0 (zero dollars, or no money) in an investment and I receive $10, my ROI is infinite.

Infinite returns are the objective. For example, The Rich Dad Company was founded with $250,000 from investors. After three years, $500,000 was returned to investors. For the past 20 years, the returns to Robert and Kim have been infinite.

Another example: I buy 10 shares of a stock for $10, paying $1 per share. The stock goes up to $5 a share, with the total value of ten shares increasing to $50. I then sell two shares for $5 and receive my entire initial $10 investment back. I now have eight shares of stock for free. Again, an infinite return.

One difference between stocks and real estate is that real estate has the added advantage of debt and taxes. Think about that the next time someone tells you an 8% return is a good return on your money.

THE REALLY BIG BONUS!

10 Video Lessons
to Awaken Your Financial Genius

Most of your friends and family won't read this book.
Thank you for reading this book.
If you want to receive… you must give before you receive.
You can give by teaching.
The more you teach the more you learn.

This is why we're created RDTV… television inside a book.

10 Weeks to Awaken
Your Financial Genius

The 10-Week Program:
Get together with three to five friends
to watch one video lesson per week,
discuss lessons from the video and
play the *CASHFLOW* game for two hours
then discuss what you learned.

TO INCREASE
YOUR FINANCIAL INTELLEGENCE

Choose Your Teachers Wisely

Most Teachers Are Great People...
but they don't practice what they teach.
ALL my teachers in Flight School were pilots.
And ALL my Advisors are rich.
They practice what they teach.

RDTV LESSONS
How to use RDTV and the CASHFLOW game to Awaken your Financial Genius

INTRODUCTION
The Story of Rich Dad:
What Is Financial Education... *Really?*
Robert Kiyosaki

LESSON #1
Why Savers Are Losers
Robert Kiyosaki

LESSON #2
Why Debt Makes the Rich Richer
Ken McElroy

LESSON #3
Why Taxes Make the Rich Richer
Tom Wheelwright, CPA

LESSON #4
How Crashes Make the Rich Richer
Andy Tanner

LESSON #5
How Laws Make the Rich Richer
Garrett Sutton, Esq.

LESSON #6
How Being Generous Makes the Rich Richer
Kim Kiyosaki

To view these RDTV Lessons visit:
RichDad.com/RDTV

GUIDELINES FOR OFFICIAL* RICH DAD
CASHFLOW CLUBS

Combine RDTV and the *CASHFLOW* game
to Awaken your Financial Genius

1: Allow at least 3 hours for each event.

2: Start on time and end on time. If people want to stay longer, that's fine. Those who need to leave have kept their time agreement.

3: Start each *CASHFLOW* event by allowing all participants up to one minute to introduce themselves and state what they want to learn from the event.

4: Watch the appropriate lesson from RDTV. For example, Lesson #3 of **How To Awaken Your Financial Genius: Why Taxes Make the Rich Richer.** After watching the lesson, spend up to 30 minutes discussing the video lesson with the people at your table. [Note: From Cone of Learning: Participating in a discussion increases learning and retention by 70%.]

NEW PARTICIPANTS

If a new person has joined the group, it is best they start by watching the Introduction Video and then join the group.

The group should spend time welcoming the new person and allowing them to state what they learned from the Introduction Video.

5: Play *CASHFLOW.* End the game 30 minutes before the end of the event. Do not worry about completing the game. There is always the next event.

Spend the remaining 30 minutes discussing what participants learned by playing the game and how the lessons they learned relate to the video lesson they watched at the start of the event.

* Official CASHFLOW Club: A club that follows the Guidelines and the Code of Honor.

6: End the event with closing remarks from the *CASHFLOW* Club Leader.

CODE OF HONOR

1: *CASHFLOW* Club Leaders agree to support the Mission of The Rich Dad Company: **to elevate the financial well-being of humanity.**

2: Keep the *CASHFLOW* Club event a sanctuary for learning. This means no selling or promoting investments or business opportunities. A Club event is not a place to be "looking for dates." Keep the event a "safe space" for learning and the exchange of ideas.

3: Do not give people the answers. Be patient. Allow participants to learn by trial and error, by making mistakes and learning from their mistakes. True education is a process of discovery, not memorizing answers or being told what to do. It's important to make mistakes—and learn from those mistakes. Mistakes are only sins when not admitted.

4: What is shared in the room stays in the room.

5: Allow each person his or her point of view. Be kind. Have fun. Treat everyone with respect.

CASHFLOW Club Leaders
agree to operate at the highest levels of legal,
moral, and ethical standards.

WHAT AMERICANS REALLY WANT... *REALLY*

Poor Dad:
"I want a safe, secure job."

Rich Dad:
"I want my freedom."

Dr. Frank Luntz is one of America's most respected communications professionals. He is best known as a "pollster," often seen on television measuring the mood of the American people. Frank is the winner of the *Washington Post*'s Crystal Ball award because he can "see" what is going on in the hearts and minds of the American people.

Frank and I met in the green room of CNBC, the global financial television network, as we waited our turn to go on air. Frank has become a personal friend and a regular guest on the Rich Dad Radio Show.

When Frank's book, *What Americans Really Want...Really* (2009) was published I ran out to get the book and read it. His work and research is essential for anyone doing business in America.

You may notice I borrowed a few of Frank's words for the subtitle of this book.

In *What Americans Really Want...Really*, Frank reports on a landmark survey he conducted in 2008 for the Kaufman Foundation, the leading entrepreneurial think tank in America. Dr. Luntz's survey found:

"It's hard to tell which has become a stronger emotion: respect for entrepreneurs or hatred towards CEOs."

He goes into greater depth why Americans hate corporate CEOs. In his survey, he asked everyday people: ***"If you had to choose, would you prefer to be...?***

80%... The Owner of a Successful Small Business You Started that Employs 100 People

14%... The CEO of a Fortune 500 Company that Employs More than 10,000 People.

6%... Don't Know/Refused

The answers to that question clearly revealed what Americans prefer:

"Building something from scratch now is held in higher esteem than rising to the top of the corporate ladder."

In other words, *what Americans really want*—by an overwhelming margin—is to be *entrepreneurs.* The problem is our educational system continues to train people to be *employees,* which is why the mantra "Go to school to get a job" is out of touch with what people really want.

Forget Business Schools

Dr. Luntz has this to say about business schools: *"So, how to equip a generation of Americans for success in entrepreneurship? Forget about MBAs. Most business schools teach you how to be successful in a big corporation rather than how to start your own company."*

MBA programs train students to be employees, not entrepreneurs. The skills and mindset of entrepreneurs are on the opposite side of the coin from corporate executives, employees with MBAs who need a steady paycheck, benefits, and paid vacations.

The Problem Is the Educational System

A bigger problem is our existing educational system. The primary reason most people do not become entrepreneurs is because they lack any financial education. Most people live lives controlled by the size of their paycheck. Without real financial education, many of our "highly educated corporate executives" have become hell-bent on getting rich by being greedy, ruthless, hard, and insensitive.

Dr. Luntz's survey finds a growing distrust of our highly-educated leaders, both public and private, which is why the American public is realizing they need to become entrepreneurs, not employees.

Simply put, many Americans no longer trust our schools, our government leaders, our politicians, and our corporate business leaders. This trend has influenced the rise of an entrepreneur like President Donald Trump, a president that does not need a paycheck.

What Americans Really Want... Really

In his survey for the Kaufman Foundation, Dr. Luntz found what Americans really want from education...really is:

81%... Want universities and high schools to actively develop entrepreneurial skills in students.

77%... Want state and federal governments to encourage entrepreneurs.

70%... Believe the success and the health of the economy depend on teaching people to be entrepreneurs, not employees.

Will the Educational System Change?

That seems to be the million-dollar question.

Q: *Can the American educational system deliver the entrepreneurial education the American people want?*

A: No, not for years. The two industries most resistant to change are *construction* and *education*. These two industries have a 50-year lag time. That means it takes 50 years for these industries to adopt new ideas, philosophies, or technologies. Compare the 50-year lag time to the lag-time in the technology industry where change occurs every 1.5 years.

Also worth noting is that education and construction industries are highly unionized, an employee culture that is resistant to any change.

Q: Why are so many people afraid of becoming entrepreneurs?

A: The failure rate for entrepreneurs is extremely high: nine out of 10 will fail in the first five years. And nine out of the 10 that do survive the first five years will fail in the second five years. That means after 10 years, only one entrepreneur out of 100 will be left standing.

Q: So what do entrepreneurs need...really?

A: Entrepreneurs need real financial education if they have any hope of surviving the entrepreneurial process.

A Tale of Two Teachers

The story of *Rich Dad Poor Dad* is a tale of teachers, one a highly educated employee and the other an extremely wealthy entrepreneur, without a formal education. The basic difference between an employee and an entrepreneur is financial education.

The Other Side of the Coin

Academic education is the polar opposite of financial education; they are on opposite sides of the same coin.

For schools to teach true entrepreneurship, a completely different school would have to be developed. For example, rather than teach students not to make mistakes, a school for entrepreneurs would teach entrepreneurs how to intentionally make mistakes, as Thomas Edison did, and then learn from their mistakes.

The U.S. Business Academy

The United States could lead the world in entrepreneurial education if it created the U.S. Business Academy for Entrepreneurs. The United States has five outstanding military academies, training grounds for the finest military leaders in the world. They are the U.S. Military Academy at West Point, New York, the U.S. Naval Academy at Annapolis, Maryland, the U.S. Air Force Academy at Colorado Springs, Colorado, the U.S. Coast Guard Academy at New London, Connecticut, and my alma mater, the U.S Merchant Marine Academy at Kings Point, New York. These academies train the military's finest officers and future leaders of America.

An example of great leadership is Dwight D. Eisenhower, a West Point graduate, a five-star general, and, in my opinion, the last great President of the United States. I personally respect him for his leadership in war and in peace.

I propose that the U.S. government create the United States Business Academy for Entrepreneurs, possibly in New York City or Silicon Valley. The United States would then train our country's best and brightest to be entrepreneurial business leaders of the future

The difference between traditional MBA programs and military academy programs is best defined by the B-I Triangle.

Traditional schools focus on training students to fill the roles inside the B-I Triangle. Military schools focus on the three elements that shape the B-I Triangle: first Mission, then Team and teamwork, and then Leadership.

On my very first day at Kings Point, the first assignment was to memorize the Mission of the United States Merchant Marine Academy. By the end of the first day, we were learning how to lead as well as follow.

Never, during the six months I spent in an MBA program, was the word *mission* ever mentioned, much less discussed. The word most repeated was *money*.

Mission is a spiritual word, a word of love, the reason for starting a business. Money is primal, a word of fear.

Self Defense

In the meantime, for people like you and me, financial education is a form of personal self-defense in a world run by greed, corruption, ignorance, and incompetence.

Financial education is like taking a karate course, personal protection against being mugged by people we are supposed to trust.

The following is an overview of what financial education is… really.

What Is Financial Education?

1. ATTITUDE: Attitude is at least 80% of financial education. My poor dad always said, "I'm not interested in money." How could he learn about money if he was not interested in money? He often said, "I can't afford it." It is easier to say *I can't afford it* than figure out how to afford something. He believed the government should take care of him. America is going bust as millions of Americans share my poor dad's attitude about personal financial responsibility. And finally, his attitude was that the rich are greedy.

2. CHOOSE YOUR TEACHERS WISELY: When we go to school as kids, we have very little control over who our teachers are. As adults, I encourage you to take the time to really know

the people who are teaching you about money. Unfortunately most financial advisors are salespeople, not rich people. And the only thing they teach you is how to turn your money over to them. Your most important asset is your mind, so be careful and choose wisely regarding who puts information into your head.

3. LEARN THE LANGUAGE OF MONEY: Learning to be rich is not much different than learning another language. When I took my 3-day real estate course years ago, I was learning to speak the language of real estate—words like *cap rate, net operating income,* and *discounted cash flow.* Today, I make millions every year "speaking" real estate.

    When I trade options, I speak the language of options, using words like *calls, puts, straddles,* and *leaps.*

    The best thing about the language of money is that words are free.

    A giant reason why the gap between rich, poor and middle class grows wider is because there are three types of income:

    1. Earned
    2. Portfolio
    3. Passive

One reason the gap grows wider is because schools teach students to work, save, and invest for earned income. The rich work for portfolio and passive income.

4. WHAT DO YOU WANT TO BE WHEN YOU GROW UP?

The gap grows because most parents and schools encourage students to live life in the E quadrant. The richest and most powerful people live life in the I quadrant. It takes financial education to live in the I quadrant.

5. TAXES MAKE THE RICH RICHER
    Those in the I quadrant pay the least in taxes… because it is the people in the I quadrant who make the rules.

TAX PERCENTAGES PAID PER QUADRANT

Tax laws are fair. Everyone is allowed to use the tax rules of the I quadrant. Unfortunately, without financial education, very few people will.

6. DEBT IS MONEY

Income
Expenses
Debt... for the poor

Assets	Liabilities
Debt... for the rich	Debt... for the middle class

There is good debt and bad debt. The rich use good debt to acquire assets. The poor use credit cards to pay expenses. And the middle class uses debt to acquire liabilities like houses, cars, and student loans.

7. YOUR REPORT CARD

Income
Poor Dad
Expenses

Assets	Liabilities
Rich Dad	

Your banker never asks you for your academic report card. Your banker does not care what school you went to. Your banker wants to see your financial statement, your report card when you leave school.

When someone says, "My banker will not loan me any money," the reason is because that person does not have a strong financial statement. If the entrepreneur has three years of strong, audited financial statements, the banker is anxious to give the entrepreneur all the money he or she wants.

If a person does not have strong financial statements, the banker is happy to offer that person a credit card.

8. THE CONE OF LEARNING

When it comes to Edgar Dale's Cone of Learning, the focus for rich dad and was very different than the focus my poor dad had.

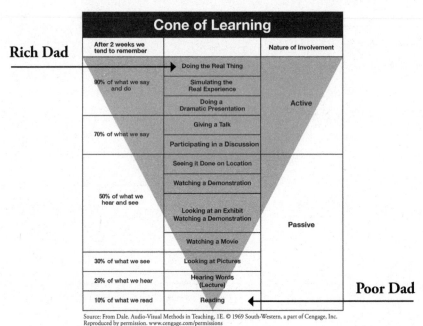

Source: From Dale. Audio-Visual Methods in Teaching, 1E. © 1969 South-Western, a part of Cengage, Inc. Reproduced by permission. www.cengage.com/permissions

Academic education is on the opposite side of the coin from the way humans really learn... really.

Twenty Years Ago

Twenty years ago, in 1997, *Rich Dad Poor Dad* was published and The Rich Dad Company was formed. The company was founded to teach the world financial education the same way my rich dad taught his son and me.

Rich dad taught his son and me by

1: Playing games (simulations), making mistakes, and learning from our mistakes using play money. Playing games requires physical intelligence, the primary way humans learn.

2: Doing the real thing, working as apprentices in his office and visiting his "green houses"—then witnessing him buy his "red hotel" 10 years later.

3: Using simple pictures—diagrams of financial statements, the CASHFLOW Quadrant, and the B-I Triangle.

4: Participating in discussion, teaching us to cooperate, respecting the opinions and wisdom of others, and not needing to be the smartest person on the team… because business is a team sport. In school, participating in a discussion and asking for help is cheating.

   Although I was an average student all through school, today I make much more money than my smart classmates who went on to be doctors, airline pilots, and attorneys, classmates who were taught in school that cooperating is cheating.

5: Inspired learning: My rich dad did not give his son and me answers. Instead, he inspired us to learn and find our own answers. Today, I spend a lot of time, at the bottom of the Cone of Learning, reading books and attending lectures. The difference is that I am studying because I want to learn, not because I need to pass a test.

Why the Gap Will Widen

Unfortunately, the gap between the rich and everyone else will only grow wider. Many of today's haves will become tomorrow's have nots. All a person needs to do is be aware of the accelerating acceleration of technology. To remain competitive, businesses are replacing humans with robots. That is why the fairytale that begins with "Go to school to get a job..." is just that—a fairytale. Rather than job security, people need to focus on financial security, and real financial security requires real financial education.

Why Most People Cannot Do It

The problem many people encounter is that real financial education is counter-intuitive. It does not make sense. Simply put, real financial education is on the other side of the coin from everything we've ever heard or learned about money. Many people who believe they are "doing the right thing" are actually "doing the *wrong* thing." These are the same people who say to Tom and me, "You can't do that here." *They* can't do it, because everything is opposite to what they were taught at home and in school.

Everything Is Opposite

1. **Rich dad's lesson number one: The rich don't work for money.** The people working for money are falling behind financially, and millions are falling into the gap.

2. **Savers are losers.** Why save money when the entire financial system is designed to print money? In banking terms, it is known as the *fractional reserve system*, which is why bankers love borrowers, not savers.

3. **Debt makes the rich richer.** The global financial system is built on debt. Money is only created when people borrow. People who know how to use debt as money to acquire assets are the richest people in the world.

4. **Taxes make the rich richer.** The tax system is an incentive program, encouraging people to partner with the government to do what the government wants and needs done. Governments do not need more employees in the E quadrant or self-employed in the S quadrant, so those people pay the highest taxes.

   Governments need more entrepreneurs in the B quadrant and professional investors in the I quadrant, which is why they pay the least in taxes.

5. **Mistakes make the rich richer.** God designed humans to learn by making mistakes. A baby cannot learn to walk without falling down then getting up. That is why games or simulations are the best way to "practice" making mistakes, learning from your mistakes, then doing the real thing.

6. **Crashes make the rich richer.** The best time to get rich is when markets crash. When Walmart has a sale, the poor and middle class go bargain hunting. When financial markets crash the rich go bargain hunting, while the poor and middle class go into hiding.

7. **Your words become flesh.** Employees always use these words, "Job security, steady paycheck, pay raise, medical plan, benefits, paid vacation, and overtime."

   Entrepreneurs do not use those words. Entrepreneurs must be smart enough to provide those words for their employees. And that requires real financial education.

8. **Become a student of subjects schools do not think are important.** The primary objective of schools is to teach students to be employees or self-employed professionals such as doctors and lawyers.

   For a person to become a successful entrepreneur, that person must become a student of subjects the school system does not think are important.

Sales = Income

One subject is sales. The fact is that sales = income. All entrepreneurs must be students of selling, always working to improve their selling skills. The primary reason nine out of 10 new entrepreneurs fail is because they cannot sell enough to survive or grow.

Donald Trump and I are the only two major financial educators who recommend individuals join a network marketing company. Network marketing teaches four essential skills required to be successful entrepreneurs. Those skills are, sales, leadership, handling rejection, and delayed gratification. Handling rejection and delayed gratification are indicators of very high EQ, emotional intelligence. Employees do not need high EQ; Entrepreneurs do.

In 1974, I left the Marine Corps and began the only real job I have ever had. Between 1974 and 1978 I worked for the Xerox Corporation—not for money, but to learn to sell. Once I became number one in sales, making a lot of money, I resigned to begin life as an entrepreneur.

In high school, I failed the 10th grade and the 12th grade because I could not write and I made too many spelling errors. Today, many people say I cannot write. Although I remain a poor writer, I make millions as a best-*selling*-author.

My Business Is Real Estate

In 1973, I took my first of many real estate seminars. That initial 3-day course has made me a multi-millionaire, over and over again. More importantly, that 3-day seminar was my ticket to financial freedom because, today, my real business is real estate.

Life-Long Learning

The biggest problem with traditional education is that many students leave school hating school. For millions of people, their education ends when they leave school. For many people, traditional education kills their spirit of learning. This is a socio-economic tragedy.

If not for my rich dad, I would have been one of those people.

Learning to sell was my entry into the B quadrant. It inspired me to become an entrepreneur—not for money, but for personal freedom. Taking a 3-day real estate course was my entry into the I quadrant.

The Love of Learning

The love of learning and lifelong education are essential for success in the B and I quadrants. Today, Kim, my Advisors, and I get together twice a year to study great books written by great teachers. The world is moving way too fast for us to stand still.

As my real estate instructor told us on the last day of class: "Your education begins when you leave here."

For most people, their education ends when they leave school. That is the primary reason why the gap between rich, poor, and middle class grows wider.

Good grades are not indicators of success in life. In fact, the relentless pursuit of good grades can cause serious personal malfunctions later in life. There is an American medical doctor who wrote about the effect of competing for a "good grade" on his life. He went to medical school in Switzerland, where there was a large contingency of Americans. He said many of the American students went into shock when there were no grades, no awards, no Dean's List, no rankings in the school. Students either passed or failed. He reported that, Some Americans just could not take it. Most became paranoid, thinking there was some kind of trick. A few went to another school, one that *did* compare and rank students, one against another. Those who stayed suddenly discovered a strange thing that they had never noticed at American universities: Students, brilliant ones, sharing notes and helping fellow students pass the course. This same doctor wrote that his son, then in medical school in the United States, reported acts of sabotage among students. He cited examples of a student tampering with the microscope of a fellow student, requiring that student to waste valuable minutes of test time adjusting his microscope. Parents are just as guilty when they demand that their little Johnny or Suzie beat their own classmates in sports or academics.

And then we Americans wonder why the gap between the rich and everyone else grows. The gap between rich and poor, smart and stupid, begins in our homes and is reinforced in our schools.

That is why rich dad taught his son and me to solve money problems as a team. We all know that it's called *cheating* in school. Rich dad emphasized that his bankers never ask him for his report card nor do bankers care what school you graduated from. Rich dad always said, "Your financial statement is your report card when you grow up and leave school."

The primary reason for the growing gap between the rich and everyone else is because most college graduates do not cooperate, they solve their money problems on their own, they take financial advice from Wall Street, and most have no idea what a financial statement is.

About the Author
Robert Kiyosaki

Best known as the author of *Rich Dad Poor Dad*—the #1 personal finance book of all time—Robert Kiyosaki has challenged and changed the way tens of millions of people around the world think about money. He is an entrepreneur, educator, and investor who believes the world needs more entrepreneurs who will create jobs.

With perspectives on money and investing that often contradict conventional wisdom, Robert has earned an international reputation for straight talk, irreverence, and courage and has become a passionate and outspoken advocate for financial education.

Robert and Kim Kiyosaki are founders of The Rich Dad Company, a financial education company, and creators of the *CASHFLOW*® games. In 2014, the company leveraged the global success of the Rich Dad games to launch new and breakthrough offering in mobile and online gaming.

Robert has been heralded as a visionary who has a gift for simplifying complex concepts—ideas related to money, investing, finance, and economics—and has shared his personal journey to financial freedom in ways that resonate with audiences of all ages and backgrounds. His core principles and messages—like "your house is not an asset" and "invest for cash flow" and "savers are losers"—ignited a firestorm of criticism and ridicule. Over the past two decades, his teachings and philosophies have played out on the world economic stage in ways that have been both unsettling and prophetic.

His point of view is that "old" advice—go to college, get a good job, save money, get out of debt, invest for the long term, and diversify—has become obsolete advice in today's fast-paced Information Age. His Rich Dad philosophies and messages challenge the status quo. His teachings encourage people to become financially educated and to take an active role in investing for their future.

The author of 19 books, including the international blockbuster *Rich Dad Poor Dad*, Robert has been a featured guest with media outlets in every corner of the world—from CNN, the BBC, Fox News, Al Jazeera, GBTV and PBS, to *Larry King Live, Oprah, People, Investors Business Daily, Sydney Morning Herald, The Doctors, Straits Times, Bloomberg, NPR, USA TODAY,* and hundreds of others—and his books have topped international bestsellers lists for two decades. He continues to teach and inspire audiences around the world.

His most recent books include *Unfair Advantage: The Power of Financial Education, Midas Touch,* the second book he has co-authored with Donald Trump, *Why "A" Students Work for "C" Students, 8 Lessons in Military Leadership for Entrepreneurs, Second Chance, More Important Than Money,* and *Why the Rich Are Getting Richer.*

To learn more, visit RichDad.com

About Tom Wheelwright, CPA

Tom Wheelwright, CPA, is the creative force behind ProVision, the world's premier strategic CPA firm. As the founder and CEO, Tom has been responsible for innovating new tax, business and wealth consulting and strategy services for ProVision's premium clientele for over two decades.

Tom is a leading expert and published author on partnerships and corporation tax strategies, a well-known platform speaker, and a wealth education innovator. Donald Trump selected Tom to contribute to his Wealth Builders Program, calling Tom "the best of the best." Robert Kiyosaki, bestselling author of *Rich Dad Poor Dad*, calls Tom "a team player that anyone who wants to be rich needs to add to his or her team." In Robert Kiyosaki's book *The Real Book of Real Estate*, Tom authored Chapters 1 and 21. He is a significant contributor to Robert Kiyosaki's new book *Why the Rich Are Getting Richer* and has also contributed to *Who Took My Money?* and *Unfair Advantage.*

Tom has written several articles for publication in major professional journals and online resources and has spoken to thousands throughout the United States, Canada, Europe, Asia, South America, and Australia.

For more than 35 years, Tom has devised innovative tax, business, and wealth strategies for sophisticated investors and business owners in the manufacturing, real estate, and high tech fields. His passion is teaching these innovative strategies to the thousands who come to hear him speak. He has participated as a keynote speaker and panelist in multiple roundtables, and led ground-breaking tax discussions challenging the status quo in terms of tax strategies.

Tom has a wide variety of professional experience, ranging from Big 4 accounting, where he managed and led professional training for thousands of CPAs at Ernst & Young's National Tax Department in Washington, D.C., to in-house tax advisor for Pinnacle West Capital Corporation, at the time a Fortune 1000 company. Tom also served as an adjunct professor in the Masters of Tax program at Arizona State University for 14 years where he created the course for teaching multi-state tax planning techniques and taught hundreds of graduate students.

Best-selling Books
by Robert T. Kiyosaki

Rich Dad Poor Dad
What the Rich Teach Their Kids About Money –
That the Poor and Middle Class Do Not

Rich Dad's CASHFLOW Quadrant
Guide to Financial Freedom

Rich Dad's Guide to Investing
What the Rich Invest in That the Poor and Middle Class Do Not

Rich Dad's Rich Kid Smart Kid
Give Your Child a Financial Head Start

Rich Dad's Retire Young Retire Rich
How to Get Rich and Stay Rich

Rich Dad's Prophecy
Why the Biggest Stock Market Crash in History Is Still Coming...
And How You Can Prepare Yourself and Profit from It!

Rich Dad's Guide to Becoming Rich
Without Cutting Up Your Credit Cards
Turn Bad Debt into Good Debt

Rich Dad's Who Took My Money?
Why Slow Investors Lose and Fast Money Wins!

Rich Dad Poor Dad for Teens
The Secrets About Money – That You Don't Learn In School!

Escape the Rat Race
Learn How Money Works and Become a Rich Kid

Rich Dad's Before You Quit Your Job
Ten Real-Life Lessons Every Entrepreneur Should Know
About Building a Multimillion-Dollar Business

Rich Dad's Increase Your Financial IQ
Get Smarter with Your Money

Robert Kiyosaki's Conspiracy of the Rich
The 8 New Rules of Money

Unfair Advantage
The Power of Financial Education

The Real Book of Real Estate
Real Experts • Real Stories • Real Life

*Why "A" Students Work for "C" Students
and B Students Work for the Government*
Rich Dad's Guide to Financial Education for Parents

Second Chance
for Your Money, Your Life and Our World

8 Lessons in Military Leadership
for Entrepreneurs

More Important Than Money
an Entrepreneur's Team

Why the Rich Are Getting Richer
What Is Financial Education... *Really?*

BOOKS CO-AUTHORED WITH DONALD TRUMP

Why We Want You To Be Rich
Two Men | One Message

Midas Touch
Why Some Entrepreneurs Get Rich—
and Why Most Don't

Best-Selling Books in the Rich Dad Advisors Series

by Tom Wheelwright

Tax-Free Wealth
How to Build Massive Wealth by Permanently Lowering Your Taxes

by Ken McElroy

The ABCs of Real Estate Investing
The Secrets of Finding Hidden Profits Most Investors Miss

The ABCs of Property Management
What You Need to Know to Maximize Your Money Now

The Advanced Guide to Real Estate Investing
How to Identify the Hottest Markets and Secure the Best Deals

by Blair Singer

SalesDogs
You Don't Have to Be an Attack Dog to Explode Your Income

Team Code of Honor
The Secrets of Champions in Business and in Life

by Andy Tanner

Stock Market Cash Flow
Four Pillars of Investing for Thriving in Today's Markets

by Garrett Sutton, Esq.

Start Your Own Corporation
*Why the Rich Own their Own Companies
and Everyone Else Works for Them*

Writing Winning Business Plans
*How to Prepare a Business Plan that Investors will Want to Read –
and Invest In*

Buying and Selling a Business
How You Can Win in the Business Quadrant

The ABCs of Getting Out of Debt
Turn Bad Debt into Good Debt and Bad Credit into Good Credit

Run Your Own Corporation
*How to Legally Operate and Properly Maintain Your Company
into the Future*

The Loopholes of Real Estate
Secrets of Successful Real Estate Investing

by Josh and Lisa Lannon

The Social Capitalist
Passion and Profits—an Entrepreneurial Journey

by Darren Weeks

The Art of Raising Capital
for Entrepreneurs and Investors